RATS, PIGS AND PRIVIES
~ A Cardiganshire Life

RATS, PIGS
AND PRIVIES

~ A Cardiganshire Life ~

ELIZABETH WHITE

CYMDEITHAS LYFRAU CEREDIGION LTD

Published by Cymdeithas Lyfrau Ceredigion Ltd.,
PO Box 21, The Old Convent, Llanbadarn Road,
Aberystwyth, Ceredigion SY23 1EY

First published: September 2005
ISBN 1-84512-038-8
Copyright © Cymdeithas Lyfrau Ceredigion Ltd., 2005
Copyright © Elizabeth White, 2005

Cover design by Olwen Fowler

Printed by Creative Print & Design Cymru, Ebbw Vale NP23 5XW

To my two granddaughters,
Caroline and Sophie.

I would like to express my thanks
to my husband,
my daughter,
Caroline Waterhouse
and Maureen Jones for their help.

~ Contents ~

Chapter 1

~ The Cardi ~

We West Walians are accursed even among our own
race; none has regard for us. We are called hypocrites
and thieves and liars. We are called 'cruel old Cardis'.
Caradoc Evans

People living in Ceredigion or Cardiganshire (as the county
was called before the boundary reorganisation in 1974) are
called Cardis and they have always been considered thrifty,
or even mean, people. This has been a source of
amusement to people living outside the area, and jokes
have always been told at their expense. One joke frequently
recounted involves three people marooned on an island, a
Carmarthen man, a Pembrokeshire man and a Cardi. At a
loss what to do to while away the time, the Carmarthen
man decided that they should pray to be rescued, the
Pembrokeshire man suggested that the prayer be followed
by hymn singing and the Cardi said he would be happy to
take the collection.

Joking aside, there is a reason for our behaviour which
is anything but amusing. I was reminded of this the other
day when a local retired farmer in his eighties, now living
very comfortably, described to me the trauma of his

childhood. He was the only boy in a family of six, whose mother had died giving birth to his youngest sister when he was only six years old. They were fortunate enough to have an unmarried aunt, their mother's sister, who was prepared to come and look after them. When he was only twelve years old his father died, of what he now believes to have been cancer. Following that they had a succession of English boys from charity homes and Irish labourers coming to work for them, none of them staying for long. He well remembers his aunt crying because she had no money to buy them food and clothing.

Many neighbouring farmers suffered the same poverty. Clothes were donated to those in need by the better off, and things that were not the right size for one family were passed to another, and so it went on. Very little was wasted. By the mid twentieth century, when conditions had improved considerably, unwanted clothes might be donated to jumble sales, which provided golden opportunities for diehard Cardis to find bargains. I remember one jumble sale organised for charity, when in order to try to clear the tables at the end, it was announced that buyers could take as much as they could carry for the princely sum of ten pence. One elderly gentleman was greatly entertained at the sight of some his neighbours rummaging frantically for more bargains to add to their bundles. 'They are all fairly well off,' he said, indicating the rummagers, and after pondering this a while he continued, 'And I dare say, this is what makes them well off.'

Nowadays, the local charity shops are full to the brim with good quality second-hand clothes, which strongly suggests that there is none of the poverty of long ago. One could call it a very wealthy county by comparison. The older inhabitants are proud to have survived the hardships of the past. Dr John Davies, in his *A History of Wales*, published in 1990, suggests that this part of the country suffered a state of poverty in the thirties almost as bad as the Irish potato famine. No doubt, we survived because we were proud people. No small wonder that the old-time Cardi is regarded as being mean and thrifty – it is the fear of becoming poor again and reliving those dreadful days of old.

As for myself, I too am a true Cardi. I was born towards the end of the 1920s and brought up on a smallholding called Parcderyn in the village of Blaen-y-groes in the south of the county. Amongst the major figures of my childhood were my aunts Sarah and Nell and my uncles Tom, Griff, Joe and Jim and their wives, especially Auntie Sally, my uncle Tom's wife, who was the headmistress of a primary school in Glamorgan. As a good Cardi I naturally agree with every word of the following poem written by Eilir in the early twentieth century and kindly translated by Mrs Maureen Jones of Aber-porth:

> *Clywsoch sôn am Sir Barteifi,*
> *Dyna'r sir y ces i 'ngeni;*
> *Cymru i gyd amdani roddwn,*
> *Lloegr hefyd rown pe'i meddwn.*

> Have you heard of Ceredigion?
> My place of birth, I chose to live
> For her I'd barter all of Gwalia,
> Also England I would give.

Dyna sir y bais a'r betgwn,
Gwisgwn hwy bob dydd pe gallwn;
Dyna sir y clocs a'r bacsau,
Sanau gleision a socasau.

Petticoats and Welsh-striped flannel
These garments I would wear each day,
Clogs and garters also leggings,
While I supped my curds and whey.

Dyma'r sir am gaws a menyn,
Ac am gawl ac am laeth enwyn,
Ac am fara ceirch a sopen,
Ac am de a'i lond o hufen.

Taste the county's cheese and butter
Go taste the buttermilk and dream
Of cawl, with leek, and bread to sop,
And cups of tea with lots of cream.

Dyma sir y cotau llwydon,
Dyma sir y menig gwynion;
Dyma'r sir sy'n dal i gadw
Yr hen iaith rhag iddi farw.

This county where the coats are grey,
Where gloves are white on Sabbath day.
Our mother tongue, and bonds that tie
Heritage that shall not die.

Sir y Cardis bia Teifi,
Clettwr, Cerdin, hithau Ceri,
Aeron, Ystwyth a'u holl bysgod,
Yn eogiaid a brithyllod.

Ceredigion's river Teifi,
Where the trout and salmon leap,
Clettwr, Ceri, Aeron, Ystwyth,
Cerdin where the willows weep.

Môn ac Arfon, Fflint, Meirionnydd,
Dinbych, Maldwyn haeddant glodydd,
Myrddin, Mynwy a gwlad Forgan,
A Maesyfed a thir Brychan,
A sir Benfro, – gwiw eu henwi,
Sir pob sir yw sir Barteifi.

Anglesey our mother county,
Caernarfon, Flintshire worthy of praise
Denbigh, Radnor and Meirionnydd,
Montgomery and Glamorgan Vales
Brecon, Pembroke and Carmarthen,
Each of these a gem renown,
But the county of the counties,
Ceredigion wears the crown.

My family were builders by trade. My grandfather was a building contractor who, besides his own sons, trained apprentices and employed local labour. When there was a recession in the building trade there was no alternative but to leave home and look for work elsewhere. There was no dole and no other answer save starvation. They would never have regarded a statement like 'Get on your bike' as anything but common sense.

Four sons went to America but only Uncle Jim stayed out there, to become a director of a building firm who built the first floodlit stadium in Canada, to the great joy of the Canadian Welsh. The news heading in the local

Welsh paper proudly proclaimed: 'And a lad from Cardigan did it all.'

We have picture postcards from all over America sent home during the early part of the century, including from San Francisco where the four brothers were part of the rebuilding work after the fire which followed the earthquake of 1906. As a child I was more familiar with the towns and districts of the United States than with much of England. We talked of Idaho, Colorado, Utah, Boston, Coney Island and Chicago as if they were just down the road.

One incident in America in particular had a long-lasting effect on Uncle Joe and Uncle Jim, judging by the number of times they told the story. They were working together in New York, employed in building a large meat smokery. For some reason or other, things went wrong and on lighting the fire after completion, they noticed smoke rising from the roof. There was no time for recriminations as the Yanks were tough people and would not tolerate inferior work. The only solution was to pack their bags and to move on, forgetting their pay.

The work was always hard, but if they were fortunate enough they might be appointed foremen at times. Otherwise it was a case of having to put up with the gaffer hectoring them all day through his megaphone, 'You with the specs get a move on,' or 'Taffy, no time for resting'. The money was good, but on returning to work in this country again, they found it difficult to settle down to the slower pace favoured here.

One of my uncles, Uncle Griff, after a short period in America, chose not to follow in his father's footsteps as a builder but instead learnt the retail trade. It was common in those days for Cardis to go to London and get involved with the milk business, in the hope that the streets of the capital were paved with gold. Uncle Griff joined this gold rush and set up shop in the East End selling dairy products. This was perhaps a more difficult enterprise in the days before refrigerators, but aspidistra leaves were commonly used to keep produce cool. Among his most loyal customers were a number of workmen, especially painters, who would frequent the shop several times a day to buy a third of a pint of milk at a time, as this was supposed to counteract the effect of lead from the paint they were using.

My Aunt Nell spent some time with her brother, Uncle Griff, in London and at one period she ran the shop on his behalf. In addition, their nieces from the Rhondda Valleys would often travel up to London to help out in the shop. These were non-Welsh speakers, the generation who lost the language because their parents moved south to find work. Yet it must be said that their English still retained a distinctly Welsh flavour, more-so than my aunt, who spoke Welsh constantly at home and had learned English only at school. Ironically, she found it easier to communicate with the Eastenders of London than did the girls from the Rhondda whose speech ran to phrases like 'where's the *clwtyn* [cloth]?' and 'Good day *i ti* [to you]', a mixture of two languages. One verse they used to recite demonstrates this linguistic mixture:

There was a great *rhyfeddod* in *Llundain* one day,
When *rhywbeth* like a lion had *rhedeg* away,
The people were frightened, a *minnau'r un fath*,
The same as a *llygoden* afraid of a *cath*.

[There was a great wonder in London one day,
When something like a lion had run away,
The people were frightened, and so was I,
The same as a mouse afraid of a cat.]

It was traditional at home in Wales to suggest that these Cardis in London were becoming rich by diluting the milk with water, although a certain amount of jealousy may have motivated these insinuations. When the great religious revival of 1904 reached London, many were moved to confess their sins and some Cardis were heard to shout from the chapel galleries, 'Please God forgive me, I have sinned, I have added water to the milk and cheated my customers, I promise never to do it again. Lord, be merciful to a poor sinner and forgive me.' Many of the rich Cardis returned to their native land after retiring, buying expensive property and living a life of luxury, but also helping a great deal with charitable work. Others, of course, failed to make a fortune in the promised land.

It seems that a Cardi is still a Cardi, wherever he may be. Some fifty years ago at a National Eisteddfod I met a couple who had come over from the States for the occasion. They were nearing retiring age, having spent a number of years as exiles. They hoped to come home and enjoy their twilight years in their native land which they loved so much and also to have the opportunity to speak the language which they had not forgotten. According to them they had gathered wealth whilst in America, through earning good money but living like Cardis.

A number of those Cardis who stayed at home through the difficult years of the early twentieth century had to struggle to make ends meet. My mother told me a very sad story about two sisters, Lizzie and Hannah, friends of hers who lived locally on a smallholding and had been quite well off when their parents were alive. As a result they had never known what it was to have to earn their own living. They were no longer young and could no longer really hope to make a living from the smallholding, yet they struggled on, although it was obvious that they were suffering from great poverty. One particularly wet summer they failed to harvest their hay as all their neighbours were desperately trying to manage their own harvesting and had no time to lend a hand. Without any help they stood little chance of succeeding but they were also too proud to admit that they were having difficulties. The result was that they were left with no fodder for the few cows they had left. Among their neighbours was a very wealthy and generous man by the name of Evan Griffith. They had been to school together and the families were lifelong friends. His barns were full in spite of the bad weather. He knew how proud the sisters were so he casually told them that he had been fortunate with his harvest and that they were welcome to some hay if they wanted it. They expressed their gratitude for his offer but they assured him that they could manage without his help. However, he soon noticed that hay was disappearing from his barn at night. At first he was at a loss to understand what was happening, but soon worked it out. One night he hid outside to keep watch, and eventually, just as he thought, the sisters arrived with a large *llywanen* (an opened sack) and filled it with hay, before disappearing as quietly as they came. There were no bales in those days and hay in the rick, as it settled, had to be cut with a knife especially suited to the job. This was hard work so Evan Griffith made sure that he not only cut plenty for his own animals during the day but also cut some extra to leave for Lizzie and Hannah to collect at night. This went on all winter but Evan Griffith never mentioned what was happening to anyone and never raised the subject with the sisters. As my mother was their best friend, they told her the story but otherwise it remained a secret.

Cardiganshire had long been a Liberal county at heart and its people were Lloyd George's people, as he had brought them their pension. However, they preferred on the whole to keep their political allegiance a secret. They had learnt this the hard way during the late nineteenth century when tenants had been evicted for voting against the wishes of their landlords, the Anglicised gentry who were often Tories. As a result, I remember during one Parliamentary election at the age of seven, being dressed in a red frock and a blue coat and told to stay outside by the roadside, as we were expecting both the Tory and Liberal candidates to pass by. The vehicles travelled slowly, well decorated in their rightful colours, and I was instructed to play a game, the rules of which were to button my coat when I saw blue appearing but to take it off completely for red. This proved more than a game for a seven year old, but an education in the ways of the world!

In those days the only obvious supporters of the Labour Party in the county were the roadmen. Although they were working class, they were often better off than a good many farmers because they received a weekly wage, and were not at the mercy of the vagaries of the market and the weather. They wore their white and green rosettes at election time and tried hard to lobby voters, with precious little success in this Liberal stronghold.

Local district elections were also very exciting occasions. Since party politics did not enter into it, they were all contested on personalities. For many years our area was represented by Joseph Jenkins, a farmer who was well liked and known for his benevolence to those in need. One of his acts of charity was to provide plenty of free farmyard manure every year for the villagers to spread on their gardens. Such was his popularity that he was returned unopposed time and time again, until the local schoolmaster stood against him and surprisingly won the seat. This was a severe blow to Joseph Jenkins, his family and the community as the new councillor would never be as generous as the old one. On the night of the election result, the family of the loser were heard crying all the way home, repeating '*Dim domin, Data bach, dim domin*' [No more dung, dear Father, no dung]. The local gardens would suffer greatly as a result of this defeat.

Chapter 2

~ Schooldays ~

There, in his noisy mansion, skill'd to rule,
The village master taught his little school,
A man severe he was, and stern to view,
I knew him well, and every truant knew;
Well had the boding tremblers learned to trace
The day's disasters in his morning face.

Oliver Goldsmith, 'The Deserted Village'

I can recall a local man, Davey John Thomas of Llain-lwyd,
saying that as a schoolboy he used to recite the Lord's
Prayer along with the other children, never having learnt
the words properly nor having any idea what they meant.
He used to repeat daily, 'Our father charred in heaven.
Harold be they name,' and so on. He well remembers
saying 'Lead us not into Thames Station' and a very loud
'Amen' at the end. Also, when studying the story of the
Flood and Noah's Ark, he was asked the question, 'How
long did it rain for?' and in all innocence responded,
'Forty-eights and forty-nines,' instead of 'Forty days and
forty nights'. Similar tales could be told by many other
children who attended our village school at Blaen-y-groes
over the years.

Blaen-y-groes Village School was opened in 1860 as a National Public School and I was greatly surprised the other day when I came across a copy of the programme for the School's Service of Thanksgiving included in the Centenary Celebrations held in 1960 – even in that year the entire service was held in English, without a single Welsh hymn being sung. This might have been because one of the old-time gentry was still living in the area and still on the school's Board of Governors. She presented each pupil with a book during the celebrations. The school was officially opened in 1875 as a Public Elementary School and from then on minutes were kept in the school's Log Book. The Log Book even details the songs taught to the children, including 'The Drummer Boy', 'Life is Short', 'Get up Early', 'The Indian Warrior's Grave' and, described as English songs, 'Men of Harlech' and 'The Ash Grove'. The poetry taught included 'The Village Blacksmith', 'The Deserted Village' and 'Owen Glendower'.

The turnover of teachers during the early years was considerable. As it was a church school, members of the governing body were selected from the local English gentry, for whom many local people worked as servants. The Welsh felt very inferior and it is no small wonder that the middle class turned their backs on their native tongue and learnt the language that gave them status. This custom can be traced back to the Acts of Union and is still alive amongst certain members of Welsh society.

The Inspectors visited the school annually and in 1878 reported:

The floor of the room is very dirty and this is probably due to the muddy state of the approach to the boys' privy. This is not so clean as it ought to be and should be attended to by the master. More pegs are required for caps. Seventy-seven scholars are marked present, though only seventy-three are actually present.

The Head must have been in trouble over this. The next year the Inspector called attention to the dampness of the floor and said it was not to be washed the night before the examination, but the Saturday before. He might well have been prompted by concern for his own shoes. The note entered for July 1886 states: 'As the room is cleared out only once a year, a holiday was given on Friday for that purpose.'

Since the use of Welsh was not condoned at school, commands were given in English and the children became used to the terms through hearing them every day. The orders 'pens down', 'eyes front', 'pass books', 'close books', were barked at them with as much discipline and regimentation as if they had joined the army. The problem with learning these terms by rote without truly understanding their meaning became obvious when a School Inspector came along and told the children to 'stand down'. The result was complete consternation as they knew how to 'stand' and how to 'sit down' but had not the slightest idea how to 'stand down'. The headmaster had to intervene to avoid total confusion.

One entry in the Log Book in the late nineteenth century states that:

It is still found extremely difficult to teach infants Object Lessons owing to their inability to understand English, consequently their progress has been very unsatisfactory. These little children hear nothing but Welsh outside the school and are therefore quite unable to attach any meaning even to the simplest and commonest of English words. A great deal of time is bestowed upon an attempt to teach them these Object Lessons, but to no avail.

These difficulties are hardly surprising as most of these poor children were monoglot Welsh speakers.

The issue of language was a persistent problem. However, in 1884, at last, a headmaster was appointed who was Welsh to the core, a North Walian by the name of William Roberts, who became very popular in the area. Patriarchal in appearance, he was both highly religious and highly interested in literature, and given to writing poetry. His wife was a very kind woman, but was inclined to suffer from occasional bouts of thirst, which would sometimes necessitate a two-mile walk to a local tavern to quench. On his arrival, Mr Roberts was somewhat surprised to find only thirty children in school, despite the fact that eighty names appeared on the Register. He soon realised that children were being kept at home for innumerable reasons and it sometimes seemed as if children only attended school when they had nothing else more pressing to do. The usual excuses given for absenteeism were 'potato setting', 'setting the garden' or 'picking stones'. Times were hard and there was real need for children to help at home, and the anglicised atmosphere which pervaded the school was anything but inviting.

Mr Roberts struck up a close friendship with the headmaster of the nearest elementary school, some two miles away. One would occasionally visit the other and on leaving the guest would be accompanied part of his way by his host. Conversation would flow freely and when it was time for the host to go home the other would turn back with him and by all accounts the two would often be out almost all night without either reaching his home before dawn.

At about this time there appeared a very odd piece of poetry in the local *Gazette*:

> Llond yr hewl hyd at y cloddie
> Yw Syr Dafi Mawr Bryndu
> Tebyg iawn fod pawb yn credu
> Mae o fwnci y gwnaed dyn
> Ond Syr Dafi ballodd gyffro
> Safodd yno wrtho'i hun.

An attempt at a translation:

> He filled the road from hedge to hedge
> Did Sir Dafi Mawr Bryndu
> True to say we all believe
> That from monkey came the man.
> But Sir Dafi would not alter
> He's a monkey still it seems.

It was obvious to the people of the village that 'Syr Dafi Mawr Bryndu' in this very insulting poem referred to a farmer named David Jones who farmed at Helygddu and not Bryndu. One of my uncles happened to be friendly with the headmaster who confessed to him that he had written the verse, having been commissioned to do so by the local councillor, Joseph Jenkins, one of the school governors.

David Jones was a very intelligent and knowledgeable person who would often argue with Joseph Jenkins, criticising his views, thus making himself unpopular with such an important person. This scurrilous verse was an attempt at revenge.

In 1897 a visitor to the school suggested 'the importance of acquiring an English tone'. This comment came from a visiting Oxford graduate, who had little sympathy for poor Welsh children. The following year Mr Roberts wrote in the Log Book, 'I find it very difficult to get such entirely Welsh children to recite English Poetry with intelligence.' Despite his affection for the Welsh language it paid him no doubt to emphasise the importance of English in order to satisfy the people who lived in the mansions and who were in charge of his livelihood.

There were, of course, topics other than poetry to be taught. In the early years of the twentieth century a local lady called Sophia Williams was employed as a 'sewing mistress' at a salary of twenty shillings a quarter, to teach needlework to the girls. She was a first-class needlewoman and was keen for her pupils to be likewise. She had one very disappointing girl whom she would savagely rebuke, saying, 'I'll hang you from the beam one of these days, how dare you sew so badly,' as the poor girl invariably pricked her finger with the needle and managed to bleed all over the material. Miss Williams was exceptionally strict and if anyone dared utter a word in her class she would write their names on a slate under the heading of 'Misbehaviour' and take it to the Headmaster.

I was told an almost unbelievable tale by my mother,

who was in Miss Williams's class, about an incident which took place the day the sewing examiner came to school. The older girls had been given a certain amount of work to get through during the year, which they had completed, but on the day of the exam they were only to show the work that Miss Williams had done. She had gone to the trouble of sewing a whole set of a year's work for every girl in the top class. Even that did not satisfy her determination to see her pupils excel.

It was known beforehand that the girls were to work on patching on the day of the exam as the teacher had been ordered to produce the material to be used on the day. She went to a great deal of trouble to obtain a piece of different material for each girl, enough to cut into two identical pieces. Her scheme seemed too complicated for words, not to mention extremely risky.

Firstly, all the girls were to have a pocket sewn into the knickers they would be wearing that day. Miss Williams then provided an almost finished patch for each girl to place in her pocket, having, I assume, made a note of which material each girl had and also having made the girls learn this information thoroughly. The examiner on the fateful day would give out the pieces of material and the girls would carry on with the work until very near the end. By then they would have, with the information already learnt and the help of the teacher, who pretended that she had to pass on instructions to the girls in Welsh, found out who had their matching perfectly sewn patch. At a wink from Miss, the first pair would ask to leave the room to go to the toilet, which was down the bottom of the yard, where the exchange of patches would take place. The girls would then return to place the last few stitches in their immaculate work. Several pairs had to leave the room in succession in order to carry out this amazing act of cheating.

The class had practised all this during many 'dress rehearsals' for weeks before the exam. All this plotting made some of the girls physically ill on the day since they were so afraid that something would go wrong and that they would be caught cheating. Was it worth the whole effort? Also, it seems inconceivable that the examiner did not see through all the intrigue. How could a class of young girls produce almost perfect work? How could they troop out in pairs like this without drawing attention to themselves? Yet they did and the ruse was successful, as my mother was able to testify.

Human nature does not change much and then, as now, girls in school could be quite cruel to each other. When my mother was at school, the two senior girls were sworn enemies and all the other girls had to choose to follow one or the other. Neutrality was not an option and the result was two distinct camps, who were virtually at war, with actual fighting breaking out at times between the two girls and their most ardent supporters. My mother was faced with a considerable dilemma since she was related to one, but had to walk home along the same route as the other. Self-preservation required her to take the side of her neighbour, although it caused her a great deal of unhappiness. The two rival bullies were both farmers' daughters and the family of one of them rented a small island, close to the mainland. There was very little growth on it so the sheep grazing it did not fatten much. This provided a first-class opportunity for the other girl to shout, 'Ha, Ha, *defaid bach hanner coronau*' ('Sheep only worth half a crown', a small sum even in those days). It was not surprising that some children displayed a nastier nature than others and one teacher believed this behaviour was a characteristic of certain families. It was probably easier to judge the truth of this theory in those days because there were so many children in each family, which made it possible to make fairly meaningful comparisons.

One way of avoiding hostility and ensuring popularity amongst one's schoolmates was by possessing a *cylch* or hoop and keeping it in motion, with the help of a stick, for long periods. Morris had the best hoop of all, the envy of everyone and it was considered a great condescension on his part to allow any of the other children to see how successful they would be in mastering the art of using it. Morris always wore a red handkerchief tied around his neck and if some of the children got annoyed with him for not allowing them a turn they would chant after him: '*Dafi Morris Toris, macyn Sarah Finch!*' 'Macyn' is the word used for handkerchief in our part of Cardiganshire, so the children were taunting him that the handkerchief he wore belonged to his family's maid, Sarah Finch. 'Toris' referred to the fact that his parents were known to support the Tory party.

My Aunt Nell had been blessed with naturally curly hair and, as a result, when she started school someone called her 'Curly'. Her response to this was to refuse to take her cap off at school. This went on for some time, despite various punishments, such as leaving her on her own in the porch during lessons (which seemed a very cruel treatment for a little girl of five). No matter what the punishment, she would not allow anyone to remove the cap. In the end they gave up trying and she decided of her own accord when it was time to submit. Aunt Nell was a remarkably neat person and I still have in my possession a lovely little metal and celluloid rabbit containing a tape measure wound and unwound by turning the tail, which was awarded to her in school for neat work and for clean and tidy appearance. Her sister, my mother, was a very different kettle of fish, who could appear quite untidy and dishevelled at times. She had, however, been gifted with a good brain and was presented with a large collection of books for excellent work, one in particular as a special prize from a visiting Inspector of Her Majesty's Schools.

In summer the children had one day during the warm weather to go to the beach, either at the end of July or in early August. This may well have been on the famous *Dydd Iau Mawr*, a day when there was almost a general holiday in the area, especially among the farming community, when they would descend in their horses and carts on the nearby beach at Aber-porth. The school was also closed for the local ploughing match in February and a blind eye was invariably turned to the children staying away from school for every auction and preaching service held in the locality.

The poet-headmaster Mr William Roberts was succeeded in 1900 by a Mr Garfield Lloyd who continued as head for over thirty years. In contrast, this man came from south Wales and was a certificated teacher. Unlike his predecessor, however, he would have made some of Dickens's headmasters look lenient. He was an extremely versatile person, who became a councillor, a choir conductor and a church music leader. He was a keen gardener, was skilful with his gun and he helped the local folk to write letters and draw up their wills.

Under Garfield Lloyd's direction, the school choir competed all over the county, winning prizes everywhere they went. Choir practice would take place at lunchtime, after school and even on Sunday if need be. If the choir had won the night before all was well, but if not the headmaster's mood would be so dire that the pupils took their lives in their hands by attending school the following day. Lloyd was rather fond of his drink and his use of the cane sometimes reflected his consumption of alcohol the previous night. His wife, who also taught at the school, was as much a victim of his moods as were the children. Yet, while he was nasty, she was worse; one boy was said to have been deaf for the rest of his days after being constantly hit on his head and banged against the partition wall by Mrs Lloyd.

There were good days at the school. Whenever the headmaster turned up in the morning wearing pinstriped trousers and shoes with elasticated sides there were smiles all round, as it meant 'Sir' would be attending a funeral in the district, as was his duty as councillor, churchwarden and headmaster. Several entries in the Log Book noted that the headmaster was absent 'at the funeral of a dear friend'. This prompted one of the governors to assure Mr Lloyd that he was a very fortunate man as he must have more friends than anyone else he knew!

One of Garfield Lloyd's first pupils at Blaen-y-groes School was Dora Anne Thomas. As Dora Anne was some sort of relation of ours, she was a frequent visitor at

Parcderyn and over the years related all sorts of stories about her time at the school as a pupil and later as a teacher. Garfield Lloyd employed her a teacher even though as a child she was constantly being rapped over the knuckles by him as punishment for her poor handwriting. There was always a vast amount of homework to do and after prayers in the afternoon Mr Lloyd would stand between the two doors, one leading to the boys' porch and the other to the girls', promising dire consequences if they did not do their homework, 'I am giving you a warning tonight, tomorrow it will be a warming.' Everyone knew from bitter experience that the warming would be provided courtesy of the cane.

As a child Dora Anne used to recite a great deal. She once recited an English poem that she had learnt at school at her chapel concert where everything took place in Welsh. After she had finished the piece the minister joked, 'That is a little English girl from Blaen-y-groes.' She sulked and cried for hours while her family tried to determine why she was so upset by the minister's quip. In the end they coaxed her into explaining that she thought being English meant being an orphan, since most English children she knew were boys sent to work on local farms from orphanages in England. The idea that her own minister associated her with these boys proved too much for her to bear. She was eventually consoled when her father promised to find an elocution teacher to teach her to recite Welsh poetry in future. After that she won many prizes including silver cups, medals and prize bags, which were given to hold any money won.

She was taken around the country to eisteddfodau by a

neighbouring farmer in a pony and trap. This farmer, Dai Llan-las, along with his two sisters, Margaret and Jane, used to compete as a quartet. Of course, one needs four to make a quartet and at one time my Uncle Jim was the fourth member of the party. He was gifted with a lovely tenor voice and he sang a great deal even after he emigrated to America. When his daughter Mildred was old enough she used to accompany him, indeed she must have been a fine accompanist since she also played for a choir of three thousand voices in Chicago. Just before he died in his eighties, Uncle Jim sent for a copy of his favourite solo, 'Yr Hen Gerddor' (The Old Singer), as he felt like rendering a Welsh solo one last time before he died.

Many parents did not make much effort to encourage their children to take advantage of their education. They wanted their children to work and earn money as soon as possible so that they could contribute to the family income. Many bright children lost out because of their parents' attitude. On the other hand, there were parents who sacrificed everything to give their offspring a better chance. Some passed the scholarship examination to enter the grammar school at Cardigan. One family from the village had four children out of five passing the examination, with three of them topping the list for the county. There were two examinations: the scholarship for those under thirteen years and the Teacher's Candidate for those under fourteen. There were three free places at the school for each area. Anyone who entered the grammar school having passed the Teacher's Candidate examination was given £30 a year, which would have to be repaid if they left school without completing the course. After passing the examination, one was expected to teach for one year. Even someone whose intention was to become a vet had to undergo this practice. Textbooks and accommodation still had to be paid for and country students had little choice but to stay in town four nights a week as there was no public transport available.

Garfield Lloyd had two daughters, called Harriet and Winnie. Winnie taught at the school as an unpaid help, in the vain hope that when her mother retired she would be allowed to step into her shoes. Harriet never sat either of the two scholarship examinations, so she had to pay for her education. Prior to her entering the grammar school one of the teachers at the local school gave her extra lessons during the lunch hour in Latin, Algebra and Geometry. Dora Anne Thomas started grammar school the same time as Harriet, but since Harriet was three years older she was placed in the fifth form and Dora Anne in the third form. Despite the extra tuition, Harriet found the work too difficult and failed the Senior Certificate.

The grammar school in Dora Anne Thomas's day catered for 250 pupils in classes of thirty each, with usually about ten students staying on until the sixth form. The Senior Certificate was taken at the end of the fifth form and the Higher Certificate at the end of the sixth. Dr Silyn Morris, the headmaster of the school, was a gentleman who never needed to use the cane to win the respect of his pupils. A neighbour of mine, who had also attended the school during his term of office, told me how on one occasion she had been accused of dishonesty in her work, an unfounded accusation which had worried her terribly. Annie May lodged in town during weekdays so she could not discuss the matter with her parents. Eventually she made up her mind to go and see the headmaster but as she did not want to be seen doing this, she decided to go to his house. Apparently she was so scared that she walked up and down the road near his home for what seemed like hours before summoning up the courage to knock at the door. She found him to be extremely sympathetic; he believed her story and promised to speak with the teacher concerned. Mrs Morris even brought her a cup of tea and a cake. It seemed that Dr Morris was rather flattered that a young girl like that had enough faith in him to believe that he would be prepared to listen and to credit her with telling the truth.

In the morning assembly held in the main hall, the boys and girls sat in files. Everybody would be talking hundred to the dozen until the footsteps of the headmaster and his deputy were heard coming along the corridor. There was an immediate hush and by the time he arrived there would be perfect silence. In those days it was still customary for children to show respect to their elders, especially to the professional people they encountered. Doctors, teachers, vicars and ministers of religion would be greeted with, 'Good morning, sir,' and there was still a certain amount of fear of the village bobby.

In that period, at the start of the twentieth century, Welsh was taught at the school entirely through the medium of English. Some of the children who lived on farms had the advantage of being able to converse daily with the English boys from the orphanages who worked as servants for their parents and this was a great help to them with the language.

After finishing the course at the grammar school, Dora Anne Thomas returned to teach at her old school at Blaen-y-groes. She quickly realised that a good teacher needed many and varied talents. Being able to draw and recite simple and amusing rhymes to keep a class of lively children entertained was a great advantage. She remembered one of the poems that she used to teach the infants in those days:

> Five little pussy cats invited out to tea,
> Cried, 'Mother let us go, for good we'll surely be,
> Spoons in right, cups in left, we'll remember
> To make a pretty bow, and never make a row.'

They were taught Geography at an early age and made to recite definitions such as 'Confluence is the junction of two rivers' and 'A peninsula is a piece of land jutting out to sea'. They could hardly pronounce the words let alone understand what they meant. In 1926 the Welsh language was at last introduced into the infants' classroom in Blaen-y-groes school. This caused considerable problems for Garfield Lloyd, however, since he could not write or spell correctly in Welsh and his wife was almost as bad.

About this time, Miss Thomas was moved from teaching infants to teaching the second class, sharing a room with the headmaster. She had already, unbeknown to Mr Lloyd and against the rules, been explaining the work in Welsh to her pupils because she felt that she was otherwise wasting her time using a language her pupils could not understand.

She was now expected to teach History, Geography, English Grammar and Arithmetic. The Geography timetable consisted of studying Wales for the first term, England the second, with all the work done being repeated during the third term. It was extremely difficult to teach two classes in one classroom, so the timetable had to be staggered. It was easier in the summer since one class could be taught in the porch or the playground to give the other class the opportunity to do some oral work.

The school was constantly praised for its results in English Grammar and the children seemed to be forever learning the singular and plural of words. They would have a spelling test, dictation and mental arithmetic test every day. Mr Lloyd was a firm believer in learning the Three R's. He was also insistent that the children should hold the writing pen in one particular way using four fingers. E J Arnold's nibs alone were to be used and no-one dared use a Jay or a Relief for fear of facing the cane. Every Wednesday the first lesson was Handwriting, when lines written on the blackboard were to be copied four times over. The type of copybook used for this exercise is still to be found in some schools today; it has four horizontal parallel lines repeated the length of the page, the two outside in blue, the two inside in red with the writing fitting into the confines of those lines.

Welsh lessons were given two to three times a week. These lessons did not involve any grammar work. Instead Dora Anne Thomas would read a story or describe a famous historical event and then the children would come out in turn in front of the class to give their own version of the event in their local dialect. They were introduced to writing Welsh gradually, beginning with writing the Lord's Prayer. Exams were held in all subjects at the end of each term and she as teacher was more afraid of the results than the children themselves in case the headmaster would give her a bad report if the results were not adequate. From everything that I have heard from past pupils this was not likely to have happened in Miss Thomas's class. She would even give extra lessons to any children who wanted them at her home after school hours. She felt so sorry for them as they suffered so much at the hands of the headmaster and were so afraid of him. It was understood that the children would walk across the fields to her house to avoid meeting Mr Lloyd on the road and having to explain where they were going and why.

It was drilled into the children that they had to be polite and never answer back. They were never rude to the staff and, with one or two notable exceptions, they were very obedient. When going out to play it would be 'Good morning, sir,' or 'Good afternoon, sir,' and courtesy was always shown to the female staff.

As the village school was a church school, Scripture lessons had to be taught daily. These occupied the first hour, from nine until ten o'clock every morning. The headmaster loathed the subject so Dora Anne Thomas had to oblige. He was actually a Congregationalist, confirmed in Church simply so that he might become headmaster of a church school. The Scripture syllabus consisted of the Catechism, the Creed and the Collect, six miracles, six parables, six psalms and the Lord's Prayer. This subject was taught every day from September to February when the inspector visited the school to examine the children. The only advantage of this was a half-day's holiday in the afternoon following the exam in the morning. It was a partly written and partly oral exam, with the older children writing out a psalm from memory and the children in Mrs Thomas's class having to memorise the Lord's Prayer. They were sometimes given the choice of writing the work in Welsh if they wished to do so, although this very much depended on the visiting inspector who was always a clergyman. A certificate was given for passing the Junior Examination and a Bishop's Certificate for the Senior Examination.

In addition to Scripture lessons, prayers were said twice a day:

Morning Prayer
> Almighty God I beseech thee to hear my morning
>> prayer.
>
> For the sake of Jesus Christ,
> I humbly thank thee for keeping me safe during
>> the past night.
>
> Defend me this day from all sin and harm,
> Make me dutiful and obedient to my parents and
>> teachers.
>
> And kind and gentle to my companions.
> Help me to remember that thou seest me at all times,
> Make me honest in all I do and true in all I say.
> May the holy spirit lead me in the way that I
>> should go,
>
> Any help me to grow better every day. AMEN.

Afternoon Prayer
> Oh, great and heavenly Father teach me how
>> to pray,
>
> Make me sorry for my faults, affecting me
>> all the time.

Give me grace to become grateful for all they mercies,
For my health, food and clothing,
Keep me from sin and danger and give me quiet,
    rest and sleep.
Bless my father and mother, brothers and sisters,
And take us all into they holy keeping this night.
For the sake of Jesus Christ. AMEN.

Teachers at the Nonconformist Sunday School noticed
that the children from the church school were streets
ahead of those from council schools when it came to
knowledge of the Scripture. Of course children taught in
English at school had to undertake some rapid mental
translation in order to give the answers in Welsh, the
language used in the chapels. It was a good exercise
towards becoming completely bilingual. Council schools
were established, but they were never made to teach the
same amount of Scripture. This annoyed me for years, but
today I am quite pleased to have had so much knowledge
of the Bible drummed into me at such an early age.

Dora Anne Thomas studied Welsh at the grammar
school, but she still felt hesitant about spelling Welsh
words since so much of her education was in English.

An old lady, Mary Anne, who was a dear friend of the
family, died recently, well into her nineties. She was
married to an Englishman who learnt Welsh having come
to work on a local farm. Although she never mastered
speaking the English tongue properly, Mary Anne would
only ever write in that language and she did it well. She
showed me a Certificate of Merit for Good Attendance
awarded to her by the school governors as she had

attended 353 times out of the 418 times the school was open in the year 1905.

The children who stayed at the local school until they were fourteen received precious little Welsh education: that was left almost completely to the Sunday Schools. Like Mary Anne, many of the older generation who are not so fluent in speaking English will prefer to write in English. The children did not learn much about local history of their own country, but a great deal about Henry VIII and William the Conqueror. There was never any mention of the Norman-built motte and bailey castle, with the mound still visible, that was located within miles of the school. The only Welsh story Dora Anne Thomas ever heard the headmaster reading to the children was the tale of Llewelyn and his dog Gelert.

The school governors were members of the local gentry, usually English and members of the Church. The vicar would invariably be one of the governors as well. One of them would turn up unannounced every month to check the register as they suspected that the headmaster marked children present when they were absent in order for the school to get a half-day holiday for good attendance. They made these sporadic visits in the hope of catching him in the act.

Every fortnight the attendance officer, or 'Whipper In' as he was often called, would visit the school to hear from the headmaster who had been absent without sufficient reason and discuss how best to deal with the situation. The officer was a gentleman who believed in persuasion rather than punishment, with the result that Garfield Lloyd, who preferred punishment, christened him 'a wet blanket'.

Absenteeism could be a problem, and even having reached school children were always eager to find excuses to avoid work. However many times a day someone knocked on the school door, the children would all shout enthusiastically together without prompting, 'Sir, somebody at the door, sir,' in the hope that it was someone who would keep the headmaster away for some time and leave him in good spirits.

People often had difficulty filling forms so the headmaster spent a great deal of time in the school porch helping them out, to the great relief of his pupils. He was a very keen gardener, or at least he was keen for the older boys to do his gardening for him. They of course preferred to work out of doors rather than behind a desk and the garden was always a joy to behold. On Wednesday afternoons, the boys learned drawing, whilst Mrs Lloyd taught weaving to the older girls and knitting to the little ones. To ensure that they made no mistakes they were taught to recite whilst knitting, 'Through the stitch, round the needle, pull it through, slip it off.'

Once a year both children and staff were invited for an afternoon of tea and sports at the home of one of the governors. The following day an essay had to be written on 'How I enjoyed myself at the Mansion' and there was a reward for the best entry. Prior to these visits the children were duly prepared for the big occasion. There would be practice for the sports and also lessons on how to behave at the table. However, despite all the preparation, on the day one girl forgot her manners completely and when the lady of the house was pouring her tea Sarah called out in a loud voice, 'Woah, Woah, that's enough.' Being a farmer's daughter, that is how she was used to instructing the horses to stop. The day concluded with the children singing for their hosts.

It was usual to walk to school, sometimes a considerable distance. All the children wore clogs and the girls usually dressed in pinafore dresses, aprons and long woollen stockings. If they got wet on their way to school there was a change of clothing available whilst the wet clothes were dried around the fireplace with the steam filling the classroom. The children brought sandwiches with them for lunch, along with tin cans of tea, which were kept warm in front of the fireplace.

The school had no water toilets, only buckets placed in a primitive building at the bottom of the yard. There were washbasins in the porches, but no taps to turn on for water. The playground was covered in mud. Most of the children arrived at school looking clean and tidy, with their clogs shining and the girls' aprons, usually made of old flour sacks, sparkling white. Going home, they were often muddy from top to toe, especially on a rainy day. Those mothers who had several children to clean up for the following day deserved every sympathy, as indeed did the school cleaner who had the unenviable task of ensuring that the place was spotless by morning.

Once a year there was a doctor's examination, at which the parents were entitled to be present. All the children were weighed and measured by a nurse on the day prior to the doctor's visit and although the children were prone to coughs, they were, for the most part, strong and hardy. Some would claim to be ill if they had not done their homework and were too afraid to face their teachers. Of course, some families suffered from tuberculosis and a number of children died from the disease. Diphtheria and scarlet fever were also killers. If a school pupil died the older children were expected to attend the funeral of their fellow pupil, even if it meant walking three to four miles.

There was some fun to be had, however, and lots of games were played at school. One of these was called 'Dandis' and was played using little smooth stones from the seashore, snail shells or, best of all, marbles. The terms used in this game were: 'gruel', 'tip of first finger', 'tip of mad head', 'oneses', 'twoses', 'threeses', 'fourses', 'send the cows', 'send the sheep', 'wash the dishes', 'lift the ashes', 'throw the swill'. It was usually played by two players sitting on the stone doorstep, or on a bench, one on either side. One great advantage of the game was that it could be played by one individual, which helped if one had quarrelled with one's friends and had no one to play with. Ball games were also very popular, balls being thrown against the wall and caught in different ways. Poor people would make balls for their children from knitting wool, unpicking old hand-knitted stockings and winding the wool strands round a bottle cork. Of course these wool balls had to be kept dry, but ball games were usually played in summer. Other popular games were marbles, 'oranges and lemons', 'hens and chickens', 'hunting the fox' and catapult shooting.

Children were very playful and mischievous even in the harsh discipline of those days. There was a clock on the wall in the classroom behind the children's desks, but no-one dared turn around to look at the time. However, if sir's attention was taken up with marking a pupil's work, another child, usually appointed to the job, would have a quick glance. A sign language was developed to tell the time, which was understood by all. It involved the lifting of fingers or the making of odd faces, all related to how close it was to play time or to the end of the school day.

Despite the fear that Garfield Lloyd engendered in his pupils, some of the older boys did find their own means of retaliation. The most effective way of avenging oneself on the Headmaster was to launch an attack on his beloved garden. One boy in particular, Jim Llainwen, was at loggerheads with the Head throughout the years he attended school. There was a grafted apple tree in the garden and one particular year it had an outstanding crop of apples on it. This tree was Mr Lloyd's pride and joy and any visitor to the school had to be taken to see the apple tree. Dire threats were issued daily not to go near it, on pain of the most dreadful reprisals and the children knew him well enough to realise he meant every word. Every morning after marking the register and setting work for his class, Mr Lloyd would set off down the garden, with his newspaper under his arm, to visit the toilet. One fateful morning, he noticed that a bite had been taken out of a large number of apples on his favourite tree. No-one would own up to this wickedness, with the result that all the older boys were caned, although everyone knew the identity of the guilty party. Jim also decided to take revenge by urinating over the onion bed. Following this, the Head gave a talk on how weevils attack the root of young onions resulting in the shoots turning yellow and dying off. On this occasion, Garfield Lloyd was well and truly beaten and Jim was hailed as a hero!

The crab-apple tree in the schoolyard was also a popular target for mischievous children. One day a small boy called Tom James came to school with the exciting news that he had a new baby sister and that she was very ugly and had absolutely no teeth. His friend, Arthur – a genius of great inspiration who would remain full of brilliant ideas until his dying day, well into his eighties – decided that immediate action should be taken. He drew Tom to one side at playtime and declared, 'We must do something about this baby.' After a moment's thought he was struck with a brilliant notion of how to render the infant more attractive:

'I know, we'll make her some teeth.'

'Yes, all right, but how do we do that?'

'Just you wait and see. I'm going to climb that tree to get a crab apple.'

'Be careful, what if Sir catches you?'

Tom James was quite worried by now, but Arthur climbed the tree like a monkey and returned with a fine green apple. At that point the bell rang for lessons and the apple was hidden in Arthur's pocket. The two boys spent their free time after lunch fashioning a set of teeth from the apple, with the help of a trusty penknife. They regarded their primitive set of false teeth as a great masterpiece. Tom James took the teeth home and, when his mother's back was turned, took the opportunity to fit the false teeth in the baby's mouth. Naturally enough, little Annie proceeded to scream the house down. Poor Tom's efforts on his sister's behalf were rewarded by being sent to bed with orders not to go near the baby in future.

On one occasion, when Mr Lloyd had been even more

of a tyrant than usual and extreme retaliation seemed necessary, the decision was made to blow up the unfortunate crab apple tree. One of the boys, whose father worked in a quarry, was able to obtain powder and fuses and smuggled these to school one day. A hole was made in the tree and the explosives planted and fired. Fortunately for all concerned they lacked the materials and the expertise to succeed. However, enough damage was done that Mr Lloyd almost lost all sense of reason. He administered the cane with such vigour that his right arm became quite useless for a while afterwards, which meant that the children could feel fairly safe for that period.

One of the older boys, Sam, who had been involved in this prank, attended the local Congregationalist Church and was to take part in the children's service by reciting in Welsh the verse found in St Mark Chapter 1, verse 6, 'And John was clothed with camel's hair and with a girdle of a skin about his loins; And he did eat locusts and wild honey.' The Welsh word for locusts is 'locustiaid' and Sam was dared to recite the verse, substituting the word 'Methodistiaid' (Methodists) for 'locustiaid'. The Congregationalist minister was highly amused to hear his rivals the Methodists being insulted in this way and the boy was rewarded with a sixpenny piece – which may well have been his aim in the first place!

In addition to his fondness for his garden, the other chink in Mr Garfield Lloyd's armour was his weakness for women. When Dora Anne Thomas started courting the man who was later to become her husband, the headmaster became very hostile towards her, constantly making sarcastic remarks. He was probably afraid of the prospect of losing a first-class teacher but eventually she became sick and tired of his attitude. She had noticed that lately he had been giving work to the children around one o'clock, enough to last them some half an hour and telling them to get on with it without bothering him. This was happening two or three times a week. On these days he would spend his time looking through the window, from which the lane was visible, before leaving the room and returning after some quarter of an hour. Suspicions deepened when village people noted that a certain lady was often to be seen calling at the school at that particular time. Dora Anne Thomas decided on a plan of campaign to cause the headmaster embarrassment. One afternoon after the Head had left the room, she left the classroom, put her hand to her mouth and ran out through the porch, pretending to be sick and on her way to the toilets. She caught a glimpse of Mr Lloyd and the lady in question in a compromising position with an article of female underwear hanging on a peg facing her as she ran out. She mumbled an apology, went to the toilet and returned through the other porch. She was never teased after this and never a cross word was spoken to her again.

Garfield Lloyd then took a fancy to a farmer's wife whose children attended the school. He used to visit the farm when the husband was away at market and the children at school. As the farm was near to the school it was easy for him to go there during lunchtime. The farmer got to know about this, but, instead of growing angry, saw an opportunity to cash in on what was going on. If he could blackmail the Head, he could get some much needed money so that they could move to a bigger farm and life could become much easier for them. His wife agreed with his plan and it was arranged that on Mr Lloyd's next visit she would see to it that he left his wallet on the bedroom floor and contrive to push it under the bed out of his sight. It was later picked up by the husband who returned it to Mr Lloyd pretending to be in a terrible rage and demanding £500 to keep his mouth shut and not report him to the school's governing body. The money was paid up, the farmer and his family soon sold their smallholding, bought a large farm, moved out of the area and never looked back.

The retirement of this particular headmaster in 1933 marked the end of an era in education in this village and the school would, thankfully, certainly never see his like again. He retired very soon after I started school so I was fortunate to be spared the experience of his tyrannical reign.

To quote a very popular and successful retired headmaster: 'I still believe, contrary to the belief of many education authorities, that it is not the number of pupils that is the most important factor in a school and that it was a mistake to close many of our small rural schools. The old Welsh village school is a complete family in itself, in fact, a cross section of a whole society. It is a way of learning how to live, to give and take as the occasion arises, as all the children will have to do after growing up.' Those words were uttered many years ago and reflect the experience of many children at Blaen-y-groes school.

Extracts from the School's Log Book 1900-1933:

Feb 23, 1900
> Ben Davies Tŷ Gwyn warned the master not on any account to touch his son William.

Feb 2, 1903
> John S Parry called to repair the school clock and took Standard 1 for afternoon.

July 3, 1903
> The vicar gave the master 3 months notice on behalf of the managers for leaving without permission and because of the rift that has arisen between him and Miss Jenkins.

July 16, 1903
> Master absent attending funeral of a dear friend.

July 17, 1903
> Attendance low. Children at the Nonconformist Festival. Register cancelled as it affects the yearly average and consequently our decrease in grant.

March 10, 1905
> Attendance poor, being that Evan Roberts, the Revivalist, was at the Methodist Chapel.
> [Many children were caned as a result, which led to a number of parents taking their children to another school.]

March 31, 1905

> The vicar relinquished his post.
> [There was hell between the vicar and the headmaster most of the time, but Lloyd's relationship with the local Nonconformist Ministers was ten times worse, mostly because of their condemnation of his love for tobacco and alcohol.]

June 5, 1906

> Whit Tuesday. Attendance poor. Children no doubt tired after yesterday's 'Pwnc' at the local Methodist chapel. [The Whitsun Festival held by the Nonconformist Chapels.]

June 6, 1906

> Master absent on important business.

Feb 1, 1907

> None of the Tyhen children in school today. Mary was in chapel yesterday and the others skating on the lake.

March 20, 1908

> O. M. Edwards HMI visited school. Complained that attendance officer was too soft.

Sept 12, 1908

> Attendance good being that the children were photographed.

Feb 11, 1909

> Sum allowed for books 3 shillings per head per annum.

Feb 12, 1909

Master absent at the funeral of a dear friend.

July 11, 1912

D. Jones and E. Jones were both employed yesterday at
the hay by two school managers.

Feb 27, 1914

The master according to instructions, gave a lecture
on St David, the patron saint of Wales, followed by
Welsh airs and concluding with the National Anthem.

July 15, 1914

Wrote to Dr Powell that he grants Certificates to
pupils who are running about at night. [Presumably
the headmaster felt Dr Powell was too generous with
his sick notes.]

Sept 8, 1914

The timetable is changed each morning to give the
children the progress of the war.

Nov 2, 1914

Master in town to see one of the local lads off to join
the Army.

Aug 7, 1915

One of the managers has presented a beehive and has
promised a swarm when it rises so that the children
may be taught beekeeping.

Feb 14, 1916

> The managers insist that the master be directed not on any account to be absent himself from school duties without the consent of the Governors.

March 6, 1916

> Acting on Board of Education instruction, the first lesson in secular instruction on the first Monday of each month will be on Patriotism.

June 7, 1916

> H. Lloyd has been acting as assistant without salary since February. [This was the headmaster's daughter, helping her mother, who was also a member of staff.]

June 8, 1916

> Miss Parry Lewis, Chairman of the Governors, is anxious to bring a charge against the master for knocking J. Bowen about the ears. It is a fact that he has for years complained about pain in the ears.

June 22, 1917

> Master absent, having been asked by the County Agricultural Committee to obtain returns for potatoes and cereals sown in 1917.

Oct 1, 1917

> New Council School opened. Their method of recruiting pupils is not creditable.

Feb 2, 1918

> Master has heard that the lad he saw off to war in 1914 has been killed in action in Mesopotamia.

April 1, 1918

Syllabus for 1918-1919. History – Hanoverian period.
Physical and Political Geography of Canada. English,
Arithmetic. Gardening. Music and Drill.

Sept 10, 1918

D. A. Thomas, an old pupil passed CWB. David Evans
awarded OBE for war service. Master absent
attending funeral of an old friend.

Oct 6, 1918

Several girls had the stick today.

Oct 7, 1918

1,177 lbs of blackberries picked in the last 4 weeks.
Children paid 3d per lb and thanked by Lady Jenkins.
Master's salary £10 6s 8d per month.

Nov 28, 1918

Attendance Officer is too lenient with absenteeism,
accepting all kind of excuses.

July 31, 1923

Aber-porth Eisteddfod. Holiday. The school choir
having developed sufficiently to compete.

July 22, 1924

D. J. Jones absent today. Last night he was taking the
Tonic Solfa Exam at the chapel.

Sept 23, 1924

Four boys stole apples. No use going to Seiat and
learning the 8th Commandment at school.

April 2, 1926

School choir won at Haverfordwest.

June 14, 1926

Choir won at Goginan. Test Piece 'Nôl i'r wlad'.

June 23, 1926

Choir won at Llanrhystud.
Test piece 'Shepherd's Dance'.

June 24, 1926

County Singing Festival at Aberystwyth. School is entitled to several days holiday for good attendance.

July 23, 1926

Master unable to grant leave of absence to Miss Thomas to attend a course at Aberystwyth next week owing to school choir competing at Aber-porth.

June 29, 1927

Master viewed the total eclipse of the sun at 6am and explained to pupils.

June 30, 1927

W. J. Jones sixth out of sixty six in the County scholarship, eleven places awarded.

July 26, 1929

Miss Parry Lewis presented illuminating address recording the success of the school choir.

April 1, 1930
>Welsh to be included in the Time Table.
>Reading Book *Cwrs y Lli.*

June 16, 1930
>Teachers ordered pupils to ring the first bell before
>they arrive. This is contrary to master's instruction
>and custom for 30 years.

Oct 17, 1930
>Told assistant that slates should be washed after
>school. She replied that school closed at 4pm.

Oct 24, 1933
>Vicar signed Log Book. No action taken against
>children who absent themselves continuously.

Nov 2, 1933
>Master sent notice of resignation to Vicar.

Nov 12, 1933
>Mr Owen, School's Inspector, called and spoke highly
>of the master.

Dec 12, 1933
>Headmaster resigned this day. School dismissed at
>3.30pm after receiving sweets from him.

Chapter 3

~ *Ministers, Deacons and Delinquents* ~

... the lowest and vilest alleys in London do not present a more dreadful record of sin than does the smiling and beautiful countryside.

Arthur Conan Doyle

The church was an integral part of village life at the start of the twentieth century. As Blaen-y-groes School was a church school, the pupils were taught a great deal of Scripture, mostly in English of course. My family, like so many Welsh people at the time, were Calvinistic Methodists and attended Seion Chapel faithfully for the Sunday services and the additional meetings held during the week. Even today a large number of eminent Welsh people claim that a great deal of their success can be attributed to the opportunities they were given at their chapel when young. The Sunday Schools were well attended, as was the Band of Hope during the week, training children to take part in concerts and Penny Readings. These resembled eisteddfodau on a small scale, but were not quite as competitive in nature. All this took place in Welsh, so whilst the schools and churches taught English, the chapels helped sustain the Welsh language.

Prayer meetings were held weekly and it was amazing how quite illiterate people could pray with great fervour, as if their words came straight from the heart. One member, a gardener at the local mansion, known as 'Gardener Bach y Plas', was a devout believer who excelled himself at prayer meetings. He would attend straight from work in his everyday clothes and would pray to the Lord in a most original fashion. One particularly hard winter, plagued by snow and frost for six weeks without any sign of thaw, the gardener addressed his Maker with the words, 'You've done it now, Lord, the ground is like adamant. We know that you own it and can do what you like with it. Magdalene and Manasse had lived in the frozen land all their lives, but you melted them. Well, come on now, do the same to this earth of yours.' After working himself to fever pitch in prayer, he invariably concluded with the plea, 'Oh, Lord remember the gentry. Through Jesus Christ, Amen.' He was, of course, employed by the gentry and knew who provided his daily bread.

Another character, George Henry, considered himself to be an expert on the Scriptures. One Sunday a stranger came to preach at the chapel and took his text from the eleventh chapter of the book of Ecclesiastes, 'Cast thy bread upon the water for thou shalt find it after many days.' The preacher asked the question, 'And what shall you find after many days?' This was naturally a rhetorical question and, as was customary in those days, it was repeated several times working up to a proper Welsh *hwyl*, being carried away by the spirit. When the preacher was about to answer his own question, George Henry, eager to display his knowledge, called out from the gallery, 'Bread and water, of course.'

It was customary for various religious meetings to be

held to offer support to those who were in need of financial or spiritual aid. At one time, a wake or watchnight, to be held at the home of the deceased on the night prior to the burial, was usually announced at the same time as the announcement of the funeral. The last such vigil in the village took place in 1910. It was a prayer meeting to sympathise with the family and to support them in their loss. Once, when a rather unsavoury character had died, a watchnight had to be held as usual. 'Gardener Bach y Plas' was present and prayed as eloquently as ever, contributing these appropriate words, 'Dear Lord and Father, we talk about sowing and reaping, but this one here [the deceased] has sown during his life what I would hate to reap.'

At the end of these services everyone present had the opportunity to view the dead in their coffin, if they so wished. It was customary to urge children to place a hand on the cold forehead of the deceased, causing them a great deal of fear and trepidation. The bereaved accepted gratefully all contributions of money or food to help them through the difficult period. This custom of presenting gifts still remains to some extent to this day. When my mother-in-law died some years ago, I was very grateful to the friends and neighbours who brought us homemade cakes to help feed visitors on the day of the funeral, as I had no time to cook. Even quite recently when a neighbour of ours died who had an extended family living at some distance, more than enough food was produced to feed the large gathering that assembled to say their farewells.

For many years, the practice was for the families attached to the chapel to provide food when there was a visiting preacher on Sunday. If he had come a considerable distance, it might even mean staying the night in the chapel house. There was always a bedroom ready for visiting ministers and a room set aside downstairs specifically for chapel purposes. The family residing at the chapel house would see to all the needs of the preacher, and in return for this, along with cleaning the chapel and vestry, they got the house rent and rate free.

At one time the lady member whose turn it was to provide food would carry it all to the chapel house to be cooked there. This practice was later replaced by the members donating money to the lady in the chapel house so that she might arrange the meals herself. The preacher would be joined at lunch by two or three deacons, so it was quite expensive for the person involved. More often than not the lunch followed the same pattern every Sunday: *cawl* (Welsh broth) to start with, then a main course of roast meat and vegetables, often the best cut of beef, followed by rice pudding and perhaps an apple tart as well, depending on the season. Tobacco was provided for the preacher as well – *baco'r achos* (tobacco for the cause) as it was called.

The whole business was all highly competitive, as were most things to do with the chapel, and it was only the fairly well-off that could take part in this ritual of feeding the preacher on Sunday. My grandmother, who took her turn in contributing, would frequently scold her sons for prowling around the chapel house on a Sunday night hoping to feast on the left-overs. They were also more than a little interested in Anne Jane, the attractive daughter of the house, but my grandmother's pride was offended at the prospect that they might be regarded as begging for food.

It was customary when the annual fair visited the area, to warn children and young people from the pulpit of the dangers before them if they attended. It was considered a trap for the unwary, from which nothing but harm could possibly come. Each year, after everyone else had uttered their dire warnings, one elderly deacon would rise shakily to his feet and repeat the same sage advice every year, 'If you must, beware of the big pockets.' The farm servants had to go to the fair if they wanted to change their place of work, as that was where they were engaged. They would make it known to the farmers looking for servants that they were available. A deal regarding pay would be settled, and there was no going back on it once hands had been shaken on the agreement. It must be said that there was little dignity in the proceedings and farm servants were treated more like the animals at a cattle mart than human beings in some of these fairs.

The deacons played a particularly important role at the start of the twentieth century before Seion had its own minister. One of the deacons who shouldered an especially heavy burden was Daniel Owen Davies, a lay preacher who carried out the chapel duties to the best of his ability. He experienced a particular problem with the Scripture examinations which were conducted annually by the Welsh Methodist Board. It was a written exam divided into age groups with a special class for those over twenty-one. These exams were taken very seriously as medals were presented for the best overall in each class along with prizes for those placed second and third. I remember receiving a few shillings on occasions as runner up, which at the time seemed far more valuable to me than any decorative medal. These exams were taken so seriously that it was not beyond some of the older candidates to resort to dishonest practices.

In his daily life, Daniel farmed Blaenplwyf, which made him a neighbour of Aunt Sarah at her farm, Bwlchclawdd. He called on her one day in a rather distressed state and was a long time revealing what was worrying him. They had a cup of tea, and the old grandfather's clock was heard to strike the hour twice while poor Daniel rambled on about the weather and other topics of little importance. In the end Aunt Sarah took the initiative and asked him outright, 'It is pretty obvious that there is something worrying you, Dan, do you want to tell me? If you do, out with it and let's not waste any more time.' Poor Daniel looked cowed and she feared that she had been too direct with him. He thrust his hand into his pocket and pulled out an envelope which he threw across the table saying, 'Read this letter.' It was a letter from the Methodist examining board asking for his opinion on the contents of a letter sent to them by another deacon, who was also a Sunday School teacher at Capel Seion. Aunt Sarah read the letter several times, unable to believe her eyes.

'What do you think I should do?' asked Daniel, 'There is not a word of truth in this letter. Esther is in perfect health. Can I accuse the head deacon of lying? What on earth am I to do, Sarah?'

My Aunt replied, 'Daniel, you must ask your own conscience for an answer, remembering that you are always answerable to the Lord.'

Daniel rose slowly from his chair saying, 'You are quite right, Sarah, I must face the truth. Still I find it difficult to believe that Jacob could do such a thing.' Aunt Sarah kept quiet and poor old Daniel replaced the letter in his pocket and left the house with his head bent low, mumbling his thanks as he closed the door behind him.

The letter concerned one of the women sitting the over twenty-one exam in the class. The deacon, Jacob Thomas, had written the letter to explain that this candidate, Esther Evans, was very delicate, had indeed been gravely ill and had made a valiant effort to sit the exam under great difficulties. In his opinion she fully deserved a medal for that achievement alone. Daniel Owen Davies was in a dilemma because he knew that this was a lie from start to finish. Whatever his ultimate decision, the matter did not become public knowledge and it was many years after the death of both Esther Evans and Jacob Thomas that I heard the story. It seems that the two had been lovers for years, even though Jacob was a married man as well as a respected deacon.

Jacob Thomas was also responsible for collecting the monthly contributions to the Rechabites. Great stress was placed on total abstinence from alcohol by nineteenth-century Methodism and deacons were made to sign the pledge. This practice vanished years since, but as a result of this early prohibition, there existed a society called the Rechabites, who believed in total abstinence and who also acted as a friendly society dealing with private insurance for those who could not work because of illness, especially chapel members. This was before the glorious advent of the NHS; yes, we who are old enough to remember darker times still rejoice in the Welfare State with all its faults. My grandfather worshipped Lloyd George who provided him with a weekly pension of five shillings a week, making life worth living for many a pensioner.

The local doctor used to hold his weekly surgery in the village at Ardwyn, Jacob Thomas's house. Naturally enough, people who regularly paid their insurance contribution, on being taken ill and unable to work, expected to receive sick pay after submitting a claim certificate, duly signed by their doctor. Yet somehow or other, sick people often found that no payment came, much to their surprise and annoyance. Jacob Thomas usually excused this on the basis either that they had not paid sufficient contributions, or that there was a temporary delay in payment, presumably in the hope that once these people had resumed work they would forget all about their claim. This happened to a cousin of mine who came to ask my mother's advice. She refused to believe that any of the excuses put forward were genuine and decide to take action. After finding the address of the Rechabites' headquarters, my mother wrote to them asking for an explanation. Only then was it discovered that the money had been paid out but that the agent Thomas had kept it, and not for the first time. By all accounts, Jacob Thomas was fortunate to have influential relations in high places, and no charge was ever made against him. However, if he had been saved from legal proceedings, he did not escape the judgement of Capel Seion. He was thrown out of the 'big pew', although he was later reinstated. Despite his failings, he was, on the whole, a good deacon, who knew his Bible through and through and excelled at calming turbulent meetings in the chapel. To compensate for his wrong doings he left his house to the chapel to be used as a manse for the minister.

Another story about the failings of deacons concerns a Sunday School teacher called James Davies who had signed the abstinence pledge. He was a popular, kind businessman who was on very friendly terms with our county councillor, a man known to be rather partial to his drink. One day a member at Seion was escorted by a friend into one of the private bars at the Black Lion, the best hotel in town, and who did he see there but our Sunday School teacher and his councillor friend. Mr Davies was none too pleased to be seen there, nor to hear the barmaid addressing him and his friend in a loud voice, 'Same as usual for both of you?' Mr Davies was quick with his reply, 'Oh, yes, a large glass of lemonade, please.' Who was he trying to fool?

Those old deacons have gone now; they were a mixture of good and bad, aware of the rules laid down for them and of the consequences of breaking them. They tried to give advice – as regarding attending the fair – but did not always follow their own guidelines, since they were mortal like everyone else and prone to occasional falls from grace. During my childhood I witnessed the downfall of two deacons who were disciplined by being thrown out of the 'big pew' and made to seek sanctuary in their family pew. What was remarkable was that both took their punishment without complaint and were afterwards as faithful to the services as they had always been. Perhaps because of this they were both re-elected the next time that new deacons were chosen.

Penderyn Fach: a typical Cardiganshire farmhouse.
Despite its charm, nostalgia cannot disguise the fact
that farming was a very hard and difficult way of life.

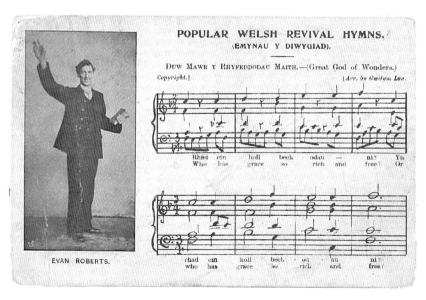

A postcard of Evan Roberts (1878-1951), the Revivalist.
This card may have been one of the 'Revival Series' produced by the
Western Mail to mark the 1904-05 religious revival in Wales.

The author's Parcderyn grandparents
with daughters Sarah, Nell and Anne.

Mamgu (Grandmother) and Aunty Nell
standing outside Parcderyn.

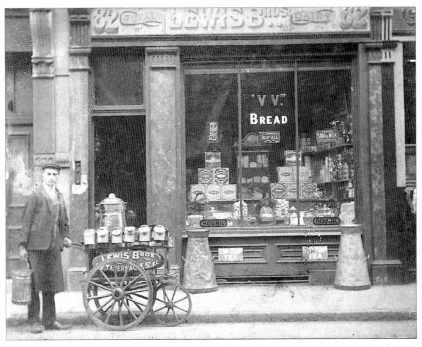

The family's London store, c.1910. Aspidistra leaves were kept in the shop to keep the produce cool, as the refrigerator's day was yet to dawn.

Builders in south Wales, including my uncles, c.1910.
The author's Uncle Tom is pictured as foreman.

The Village Smithy

Tell J. M. we failed to catch cochin yesterday

A postcard reference to 'Cochin' [*sic*] (Ginger), the postman.

'Gardner Bach y Plas' ('The Mansion's Little Gardener'). A fervently religious man who was in his element in prayer meetings.

Dr J Powell (1850-1917), a beloved physician who practised as a family doctor in the region.

Aunty Nell (standing) and friend home on holiday from London, both dressed in their Sunday best.

Uncle Jim and Uncle Joe (second and third from the left) enjoying their leisure time in the USA. Four brothers went to San Francisco to help re-build the city after the great fire that followed the 1906 earthquake. More of their leisure time in the USA is portrayed on the front cover of this book.

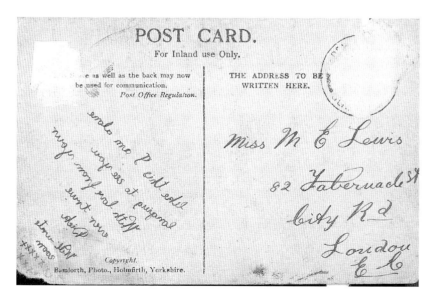

A card from Jack to Nell in 1907. Note the back-to-front writing.

A butter-making class in Plas Glanaber, c.1920. Butter clapped at home was always said to taste better than class-made butter.

The 'bando', the iron hoop's, tyring platform.
'Bando' day was special. The iron hoop tyre, once heated red-hot, would be lifted from the fire and dropped over the wooden wheel held fast on a tyring platform. Cold water was poured on to douse the ensuing fire and to shrink the metal tyre tight around the wheel.

One of the old privies which remains standing.
It was in such a privy that I had my first encounter with a rat!

The pigsty; a mainstay of Cardiganshire rural life.
Some people believed in an all-night vigil the day before killing the pig,
in case such a valuable creature would come to harm – or even disappear.

A certificate for good attendance at the local school in 1905.
Truancy was always a major problem, and getting children
to attend school regularly was extremely difficult.

A Christmas card to
Aunty Nell from an
admirer in the army:
*'Gwell Angau
Na Chywilydd*
[Better Death
Than Shame].
With Christmas Greetings
for 1917, in the Confident
Hope of a Victorious 1918,
from D. Lloyd
38th (Welsh) Division.'
The opening line of 'Hen
Wlad fy Nhadau', the
Welsh national anthem,
is on the cover.

Back cover picture:
Capel Seion's
Band of Hope, c.1900

Ministers of religion were generally considered to be middle class, although they were usually paid a meagre wage by their chapels. The first minister of Capel Seion, the Reverend Eliseus Jenkins, arrived in 1911 and was perhaps more fortunate than most in having married a wealthy woman, several years his senior. They lived in a large house rented by the chapel as a manse. Mrs Laura Jenkins considered herself to be considerably superior to her husband and employed a local girl to assist with the housework. Mrs Jenkins was, however, deemed to be an excellent cook and entertained on a lavish scale. To do her justice, whoever called at the manse was always offered a cup of tea and a bite to eat no matter what time of day. One Sunday morning Eliseus Jenkins arrived late for his service at Seion without his wife. He looked quite sombre on his arrival and had fewer friendly words than usual to say to his deacons before ascending to the pulpit. He hurried through the initial part of the service, reading the last chapter of the Book of Proverbs, praising the wonders of a good wife, and he took the text for his sermon from verses 10-12 of that chapter, 'Who can find a virtuous woman for her price is far above rubies. The heart of her husband doth safely trust in her, so he shall have no need of spoil. She will do him good and not evil all the days of her life.' Eliseus Jenkins seemed very agitated and on the verge of tears. There was obviously something on his mind and that something had to do with his wife.

At the end of the service the members were asked to remain behind. The minister then proceeded to explain what was bothering him. 'I'm very sorry to have to address you regarding a matter which has caused me great concern. My wife has been sorely hurt. It has come to her ears that some of you have been complaining that you have had shop jam with your bread and butter when you have been to tea at the manse, but that her important friends get homemade jam. And you know very well what a marvel the wife is at making jam. This accusation is totally unjust; she would never dream of doing such a thing. I tell you, shop jam never comes through the door of the manse. Jane the maid is a witness to that. Mrs Jenkins has been crying all night and she could not face coming to the service this morning.'

He then sat down with the tears flowing. Jacob Thomas rose to his feet and in his own diplomatic way tried to allay the storm that was brewing. Although the deacons went to apologise to Mrs Jenkins on behalf of their malicious and unfair members, things were never the same again and the Jenkinses did not stay long after. He was a caring minister, a good musician and one who worked well with the youth of the chapel, but unfortunately he was completely under his wife's thumb. Capel Seion lost a good minister in the Reverend Eliseus Jenkins because of jam.

Seion's next minister was a young bachelor who was newly demobilized after serving as a chaplain with the forces in the First World War. The Reverend Griffith Beynon was an extremely lovable character, full of life and mischief. He was a first-class preacher, as one of his members acknowledged, 'Keep G.B. in the pulpit and there's nobody better. Just remember never to allow him to get down from there.' At his ordination service a deacon representing his home chapel in the Valleys of south Wales whilst speaking on his behalf kept on repeating, 'What a wonderful mother he has, what a wonderful mother.' The congregation present felt increasingly sorry for his poor father who seemed to be shrinking by the minute, hemmed into the corner of a pew by what looked like a rather powerful wife.

Griffith Beynon visited his flock regularly, indulging his love of food at the same time. On one occasion he had been invited to supper at Ffynnon-oer farm, and, knowing this family, one could well imagine the fine feast that had been prepared for him. On his way he paid a visit to Dolarian, where the household were about to sit down to eat. The minister was naturally invited to join them and the appetising sight of the fresh salmon on the table proved too much of a temptation to be resisted. After a filling meal at Dolarian, Griffith Beynon went on to the substantial supper which awaited him at Ffynnon-oer. It was late that night when Aunt Nell went out to shut the hen-house door that she heard some odd noises coming from the road on the other side of the hedge. Peering through the hedge, she found their dear minister being sick along the roadside. It had all become too much for his overstrained stomach.

When Reverend Beynon was invited for a meal, his normal practice was to visit the kitchen to entertain the ladies and watch the meal being prepared. If the menu included cooked meat, he would then make a request for the outside slice as he liked his meat well done, surrounded by a crisp layer of fat. Despite all those calories he lived a healthy life to a ripe old age.

It was unheard of in those days for people to lock their doors whilst they went about their daily chores outside in the garden or on the farm, and they would rarely bother even to close their doors. As a result, members of Seion soon became accustomed to frequent unheralded visits from their minister. On his first visit to our house, he succeeded in terrifying Aunt Nell when she returned to what she thought was an empty house, after having being out in the garden, only to find it full of the smell of tobacco, although there was no-one in sight. She proceeded into the next room through the open door to be pounced on by GB with loud peals of laughter. This soon became known as his common practice. He was a good singer and a first-class mimic. An uncle of mine who was bedridden for years used to look forward eagerly to the minister's visit. He would imitate other preachers and the singing of some of the characters in the chapel, with quite merciless accuracy.

With all his high spirits he was loved by all. However, he left the chapel unexpectedly after a period of ten years. There were apparently two reasons for this. Firstly he fell in love with a very beautiful girl called Letty, but she refused to marry him because she was tall and slim and he was short and plump. I understand that this was an important factor in choosing a partner in those days. Also, he left just before the scandal over Jacob Thomas and the Rechabite insurance money. He apparently had been warned what was coming, felt that the trouble in store was too much for him and that he was better away from it all. He was a great loss to the chapel and the community. It was the Reverend Griffith Beynon that christened me and he would always call to see me and my family when in the area. He kept his humour to the end, but died a bachelor.

The chapel was without a minister for many years after

this. During this period we had to face considerable unpleasantness from poison pen letters. About this time a retired widower called Moses Llewelyn came to live in the village. He married a local spinster called Bessie Davies and both were faithful members at the chapel. Late in life he started to send rather nasty, but signed, letters to local people, a habit which became an obsession with him. His victims were mainly business people and he would complain about the way they ran their businesses. Looking back it was probably the beginning of the illness which eventually killed him that made him do this, as normally he was a very pleasant man. I honestly believe that it was this habit which unfortunately inspired certain ladies in Seion to write anonymous letters.

A wealthy farmer called Samuel Hughes had decided to retire to the village and as he was a widower he engaged a housekeeper, Martha Davies, who was not a local woman. She was formidable and very capable and became a very faithful member of the chapel. She was soon made a Sunday School teacher and threw herself into all chapel activities. I recall one such occasion with embarrassment to this day. During the war, we had been allocated an extraordinarily mischievous evacuee by the name of Martin Charles. He was about ten years of age, a little younger than me, and was placed in Miss Davies's Sunday School class. At Christmas time, the children had their annual Christmas tea and concert and after their tea they were (unwisely perhaps) sent out to play in the dark whilst the adults had their meal. The dish-washing was undertaken by Martha Davies. Above the sink in the vestry kitchen was a small window with the top section left open.

As she bent over the dishes in the sink, a hand came in, took hold of a handful of hair and pulled for all its worth. When Miss Davies screamed loudly the hand vanished. There was no need to ask who the guilty party could be, but I felt some relief to realise that Martin could not have reached the window without someone else lifting him up and holding him in position and I was by no means the only one with a red face.

Next door to Martha lived two sisters, Kitty and Lily, both widows, one quite wealthy. They both seemed to be sweet old ladies and the three women became the best of friends. In no time at all, anonymous letters were received by all sorts of people connected with Capel Seion. Samuel Hughes did not attend Capel Seion as he was an Anglican and he was one person who did not receive a letter.

A friend of ours, Hetty Ellen, was a faithful member. She was a widow who had retired from farming and had brought her two unmarried farm servants to live with her as they had no families of their own and had found work locally. The arrangement seemed to work very well and it appeared to be a very happy household. One of the men was a very popular member of the community who participated in all local activities, although he was a Baptist and not a Methodist. The other had come to work in the area at the age of fourteen from one of Dr Barnado's homes and was slightly retarded. Hetty Ellen was a very jovial person and there was a good deal of banter and leg pulling between her and Samuel Hughes. She received one of these anonymous letters stating how disgusting her behaviour was, living with two men, and one of them a deacon in the Baptist chapel too, and not content with that, here she was chasing a third man! The recipients of the anonymous letters were mainly unmarried, widows or widowers in the age group of fifty to seventy. The frequency of these malicious letters meant some form of action had to be taken. By now, people had begun to suspect who the culprits were. The handwriting showed certain recognisable characteristics, and information was divulged which was only known to certain people. On the basis of these clues Samuel Hughes confronted the three ladies, the two dear sisters, Kitty and Lily, and Martha the housekeeper, who confessed to their wrongdoing. Martha was dismissed immediately and she returned to her native village in disgrace. Jealousy was the root cause of it all since Kitty was keen to marry Samuel Hughes, but he seemed far too friendly with other eligible women in the area for her peace of mind. His housekeeper, being new to the area, had not realised how malicious these seemingly sweet and innocent sisters could be. They had tricked her into writing the letters, because her handwriting was not so easily recognised as theirs by local people.

Unpleasant events were not unusual in the history of Capel Seion. My own worst experience came when I was in my early teens. My friend Mary and I often used to walk through the woods to the nearest beach, a couple of miles away. On one particular Saturday we found it almost deserted, although it was a beautiful summer day. The days when it was possibly to have a lovely sandy beach all to oneself are long gone. I said almost deserted because there was a man in the water when we arrived, although we took very little notice of him. We chose a suitable spot to sit and sunbathe and saw no sign of the swimmer's clothes anywhere near. We were busy talking but after a while noticed a middle-aged man coming out of the water and looking in our direction, then walking across the beach away from us. We thought nothing of it. Soon he was coming back again, still in his bathing trunks and carrying his clothes under his arm. He sat on the rocks quite close to us, which we thought rather odd as there was such an expanse of beach and rocks for him to find a private spot to dress. Naturally, we were quite inquisitive by then. He took his trunks off, without bothering to cover himself with his towel. We were still pretending not to have noticed him, but this was not good enough for him. His next move was to cover his bottom half with his towel and walk towards us. We gave him the benefit of the doubt, thinking that he was coming over to chat, but when we looked in his direction he immediately removed the towel and exposed himself. We looked away as if nothing had happened. He remained there for some time but eventually had to return to his clothes. Every time we stole a glance in his direction he was looking at us as if ready to repeat the performance at the slightest prospect of an audience. He left the beach before us, dressed in a very sober black suit. Country youngsters were not easily shocked, as we were used to seeing nature in the raw, but we were still surprised that a man who appeared so respectable could behave like that towards two young girls. However, we decided not to tell anyone about our unfortunate experience.

The next day was a Sunday and we had *Cyrddau Mawr* 'Big Meetings' at Capel Seion, which meant two sermons in the evening, the first from a local preacher and the second by a guest preacher, usually an eminent figure in the

Methodist world. The chapel was full to overflowing and when we rose to sing the first hymn, who was with the deacons in the big pew when they turned around to face the congregation? None other than our friend from the beach. I was so shocked and disgusted that I did not know where to turn. He ascended the stairs to the pulpit as the guest preacher and gave an eloquent sermon. He was a celebrated Welsh Methodist minister (one of the *hoelion wyth*), highly thought of as a great preacher and a shepherd of his flock. Mary was saved this ordeal as she attended the Anglican Church. We discussed it afterwards and decided that it would be useless to tell anybody since no-one would believe us, least of all our own families. It would be his word against the words of two silly teenagers with too vivid imaginations. In fact we were convinced that we would be in great trouble if we dared tell anybody in authority. He had been staying with friends over the weekend and they lived close to the beach. They were influential enough to have shut us up pretty soon had we made any accusations. We kept our secret for years, but it probably affected me more than Mary, who was not a Methodist.

There were some characters who made use of the church when it suited them. One dubious local character was George James, the son of a farmer who lived on the banks of the river Lleu, renowned for its salmon. He came from a fairly ordinary, but devout, family, the father being a deacon at the local chapel. George never saw an evil deed being carried out at his parents' home. They even carried out family devotion prayers there (*dyletswydd deuluol*), as was customary with certain families, besides attending a place of worship three times on Sunday, as well as all the weekly meetings. George was one of four brothers, but it became apparent very early in his life that that he was far more trouble than the other three. He proved difficult at the village school. As he grew older the female teachers became afraid of having to deal with him when the headmaster was away. Once he lifted his class teacher off the floor and put her inside the large guard surrounding the fireplace and kept her there for some time in the intense heat. She was very small and he had grown to be a big, strong lad. Neither education nor punishment had any effect on him. He showed no interest in schoolwork and he would spend his time in class being obstructive. One of his favourite tricks was to hide rulers and the headmaster's canes inside the harmonium, which stood with its cloth against the partition separating the school's two rooms. There was a narrow gap in the wood panels at one point, large enough for John to force the sticks and rulers through. No wonder strange noises were heard coming from the harmonium when it was played! The staff were more than glad when George left school at fourteen.

His heart was on the river and his favourite pastime was fishing. He started work by helping his father on the farm during the day, but spent his nights on the river. This area was well known for its coracle fishing with nets. It did not take George long to master the coracle. This traditional form of fishing was dying out, and only a few people still had a license. As George failed to get one, he turned to unlawful methods of fishing, and was at war with the water bailiffs for the rest of his life. George soon gave up farming as he disliked the work, which probably did not offer enough excitement. He found casual work as a labourer, travelling from place to place. He started to drink heavily, but was never short of money, as he was able to sell what he caught poaching on the river to contacts he met at public houses.

He married one of the prettiest girls in the area, much to her parents' dismay. After Bethan gave birth to three lovely girls and after a turbulent married life, George turned his back on his family. It is unlikely that his wife missed him very much. He was well known as a strong, violent man, especially under the influence of drink.

George made fools of the water bailiffs on several occasions. One day he went to the nearest town carrying a car tyre in a sack, having first rung the police from the village, pretending to supply information that George the Poacher was waiting for the bus to town, carrying a salmon in a sack under his arm. He duly arrived in Llan-boyr and walked up the street to be met by two constables and the water bailiff. They felt jubilant indeed and confident of success. They were practically dancing with joy until the joy turned to bitter disappointment and humiliation when they opened the sack and realised that they had been tricked once more. George went away with a broad smile on his face and the policemen and the water bailiff with egg on theirs. He was not to be caught that easily and he proved too much of a fox for the local constabulary.

He then found employment with a new company which had just moved into the area and he enjoyed great success there by presenting the bosses with salmon. They were Englishmen who knew nothing of local custom or of George's character. On one occasion he was seen walking towards the office with a parcel under his arm which was opened just enough for a glimpse of the duck's head within. The theft of a duck from a local farmer would serve well to ingratiate himself with his new masters. For weeks after this event wherever he went the faint sound of 'quack, quack' would follow him, although nobody dared mock him to his face for fear of ending their days in the river.

'Salmon paste' made from salmon roe was extremely successful as a bait, despite the fact that it was illegal to either use or sell it, since its production entailed killing the salmon to obtain the roe. George thought of a brilliant idea to make money and to fool people. He mixed putty, red lead and ordinary fish paste and sold it on the black market for a high price. I have no idea how successful it proved or if anybody returned for more.

He would spend considerable time hiding in nooks and crannies by the water rather than be caught poaching. One Sunday the bailiff was convinced that he had seen George on the river in a coracle and landing with something under his arm, but by the time the bailiff had reached the road to meet him he was nowhere in sight. When questioned about his activities he had a ready alibi, insisting that he was in chapel at the time. He had not darkened the doors of a chapel since childhood, but this night George had sneaked in to the back pew in order to avoid the water bailiff. When the congregation rose to sing, George's father turned with the other deacons to face the congregation and his wayward son. The honest father swore that his son had been present throughout the service, thus unwittingly helping him escape justice, which had been George's sole aim in attending chapel in the first place.

George died before reaching middle age, having damaged his health by spending so many nights on the river poaching. One wonders whether his family were in some sense relieved to see him safe out of harm's way. There is no doubt, however, that it was the water bailiffs who sang the loudest at his funeral.

Chapter 4

~ *The Beasts of the Field* ~

For thou shalt be in league with the stones of the field, and the beasts of the field shall be at peace with thee.

Job 5: 23

Farming was the main occupation in our area, and it was a back-breaking and frequently unrewarding business for tenant farmers and farm workers.

In 1914 the Government offered farmers a grant to keep a pedigree bull to improve the stock. Up till then only the gentry kept bulls on their farms and they would allow the tenants to use them for their cows. This grant proved to be very popular in Blaen-y-groes and when a meeting was called around sixty people turned up to form a Bull Society. The importance of acquiring a first-class animal with a good pedigree was stressed. The popular breed at the time was the Shorthorn, a dual-purpose cow that could produce milk and could be fattened up for the beef market as well. Frequent meetings of the society were necessary, some of them more heated than others. It was eventually decided to send a deputation to a sale in Penrith, where the best Shorthorn bulls were sold.

It was no easy task to decide who should be given the responsibility of attending a sale and buying the bull. Having got over this hurdle, the next one proved even more difficult, namely who was to keep the bull and see to his customers? When the bull eventually arrived it was given a regal welcome at Blaencwm farm. Members were asked to pay a membership fee and then an additional payment for every cow served. The bull cost a small fortune to feed as he had a voracious appetite. Financial problems reached crisis state, until in 1924 a sale of work and a concert had to be arranged to raise funds. All this raised the large sum of £100, which solved the problem for the time being. As a child, I saw many a cow being led down the main road and along the lane to meet Samson. Our cows had only to be taken the few yards down the road, and having entered the lane leading to the farm, they would run all the way to where their suitor was waiting, some 400 yards away. There was plenty of time to follow at a leisurely pace and, perhaps, if the farmer happened to see her coming, he would fetch Samson out of his shed and it would be all over before we arrived and the cow quite willing to return home quietly.

Although the Milk Marketing Board was established in 1933, it did not operate in this area until 1936, when a collecting depot was set up near the railway station at Newcastle Emlyn. The Shorthorn was replaced with the Friesian cow that gave a better milk yield, so 1944 saw the last of the Shorthorn Society bulls. The establishment of the MMB did a great deal to improve the life for the few farmers who were brave enough to take advantage of the scheme. Selling milk every day meant a regular monthly cheque, however small. We, with only three cows, were one of the first to join. I believe that we were paid sixpence a gallon, which was a small fortune.

One of the conditions of selling milk to the MMB was to provide a suitable place for the churn containing the milk to be kept cool prior to its collection. We set up a prefabricated shed, six foot square, outside the cowshed, with a small tank of water to hold a partly immersed churn. The churns were taken along rough country lanes in the open lorries on their way to the depot. The milk was tested there, and if found to be sour would be returned to the farmer the following day and left on his milk stand, along the roadside at the end of the farm lane. Not only was this a financial loss but a disgrace as well, as bacteria acting in fairly warm conditions was responsible for the milk turning sour. If a churn was seen on a milk stand late in the afternoon with a label attached to it, news would soon get around that so-and-so had dirty milk!

Soon after we had commenced selling milk we had a sick calf on our hands which had to be separated from the milking cows to prevent infection. There was enough room in the cooling shed and we saw no reason to waste the available space. Almost unbelievably, the milk inspector decided to pay us a visit the following day, of all days. We were fortunate enough to see him approaching the house and in no time at all we all hid behind the garden hedge, with the cowshed and cooling shed in full view. He had a thorough look around but failed to see any of us. Immediately following his departure the calf was found alternative accommodation and the shed scrubbed clean and disinfected. The inspector returned the following day to a friendly welcome and he could find no fault with our set-up. The previous day was not mentioned by anyone. We found out afterwards that he had visited several farms who were housing farm animals in their cooling shed. We had learnt our lesson that the MMB instructions had to be obeyed at all costs.

One farmer described his existence throughout the thirties as 'killing a mouse and eating it'. This poverty made care for precious animals of the utmost importance. I remember how every night one of us had to go out to the cowshed to put the cows to bed. They were given their last feed and drink of the day and were made comfortable for the night on a thick bed of straw. As one entered the cowshed carrying a hurricane lamp, sometimes the noise of scurrying feet would indicate the presence of rats. The place was far from elegant but it certainly was comfortable, a far cry from the ultra-modern buildings of today. Had it not been for the rats I would not have minded spending a night out there on a cold and frosty night. It was very cold in my bedroom, cold enough to freeze the contents of the chamber pot under the bed, whilst in the cowshed the heat from the cows, along with the clean straw bedding, was very tempting indeed. It is possible that those farm servants who had to sleep in stable lofts were far cosier than their masters indoors.

Our cows were thoroughly spoiled and always hand milked by my mother, who used to carry on a conversation with Seren, the eldest of the three. My mother was a very healthy woman who went for nearly thirty years without seeing a doctor and then only when she was involved in an accident whilst in her seventies. Once, she went down with influenza and I was expected to do the milking instead of her – not the most enjoyable of tasks, but it had to be tackled. Seren could kick as well as any cow and even my mother had to tie her legs before milking. She did not like me at all and, in addition to her relentless kicking, even with her legs tied, she refused to let her milk down. It was a complete disaster and I was at the end of my tether. Having suffered two days of this, with my mother putting all the blame on me, a friend of mine came up with a brilliant idea. 'What about impersonating your mother and dressing up to look like her?' I worked hard at this, wearing an old beret over my head which covered most of my face, with a big apron made out of an old sack covering most of me and clogs on my feet. Their heavy tread announced my arrival. I also wore my mother's dark-rimmed spectacles which did not exactly help me to see what I was doing. I had no problems in tying her feet and we had some sort of conversation and in no time milk was flowing into the bucket speedily enough to form froth on top. I was never as good a milker as my mother, but she had far more practice than me. Seren remained docile although she kept peering back at the sight of me perched on the milking stool. She seemed rather suspicious of me and neither of us was sorry when my mother resumed her duties in a couple of days.

The cows would usually rush into the cowshed to be milked knowing that there would be a feed waiting for them in the manger, usually 'Uveco' and 'cake nuts' with sometimes a few chopped potatoes and mangolds added. They would pass the clothesline taking no notice even if there were clothes out. However, when Aunt Nell came home on holidays from London and her clothes were drying on the line, one cow would make a beeline for hers and start munching them. When it happened the first time the cow was excused, but when it happened the second time everyone was perplexed. No-one came up with a plausible explanation, so the only solution was to keep Aunt Nell's clothes off the line during milking time.

One of the most important events of the farming calendar was haymaking, which required a great number of helpers. Bales were unheard of before the Second World War. Instead the hay was carried into the barn in the farmyard and made into a rick. To start, the hay had to be collected in the field with hand rakes – work which was allocated to women – then pitched with pitchforks onto the horse-drawn carts. Some strong healthy women would take on this task as well, but it was generally a job for the men. It was usually done in pairs, to load as much as possible in one go. The women would follow, raking what was left so that none should be wasted.

One person managed the cart, unless a big 'gambo' was used when two people would be needed. This was also an important job as considerable skill was needed to make a well-balanced load that would not topple over when the horse and cart were driven over rough ground. There would be several carts involved so the people forming the rick were kept busy. A young lad would usually lead a horse back and fore to drive the mechanical pick, which picked the hay off the carts, took it up to the top of the shed, guided it along and let it down where required. There would be several people in the shed to receive the hay and form the rick. This was quite a skilled job and required one or two experienced men to guide the others, who often included women.

Sometimes the young lad leading the horse would get fed up and go on strike and would have to be cajoled or bribed to carry on. On some farms the fields could be far from the homestead and it took time to bring in the load. One farmer who liked to give the impression that he was highly successful used to instruct his workers not to fill the carts too full so that he could brag in the pub how many loads per acre his hayfields were yielding. Most people would know his game and they also knew that he was the worst farmer in the area!

Food was the best part of haymaking and as children we were always willing to volunteer for work knowing that the reward would be in food. For tea it was bread and butter, both brown and white, with cheese, fruitcake, *bara brith* and Welsh cakes, all home-made. Everything tasted so much more appetising eaten out of doors. For supper it was sandwiches with boiled new potatoes, a selection of cakes, and on some farms the wife would even produce an apple tart to try to beat her neighbours. It seemed that Welshmen were very partial to apple tart. My mother joined in the competition and produced the apple tart when our little bit of hay was harvested. Tea was made in a *shwc*, a tin-plated gallon can with a lid to it, which shone beautifully and was only used at harvest time. For the rest of the year it hung from the beams in the kitchen along with the bacon. Making tea for so many was a complicated business. Having ascertained how many people would be partaking and calculated how many spoonfuls of tea were required, the tea was placed in a muslin tea bag, tied with a string and lowered into the *shwc*. An estimated amount of boiling water was added and after allowing time to brew and giving it a good stir the teabag was removed and milk and sugar added. The actual amounts were settled by trial and error. After the first addition, anyone within reach was used as a taster. In the end a compromise was reached, taking the views of the tasters into consideration. There was little problem in those days of some not taking sugar and some not taking milk. On the rare occasions that this happened, the individual was expected to declare his or her special request to the farmer's wife on arrival.

Corn harvesting was also a busy time for the farmer. It was only the larger farms that grew grain – mostly oats as the climate was too wet for wheat and barley, especially wheat. In the early days the corn was cut with scythes; the men starting at the crack of dawn and carrying on until dusk, as long as the weather held. The introduction of the binder was a great step forward; it not only cut the corn but also tied it into sheaves. It was followed in the field by a number of workers lifting the sheaves off the ground and placing four of them to stand up against each other to make shooks, with their bases spread out and their tops, the grain end, close together; this was done to dry them out completely. This process was called *stacano*, and it was followed by *sopino*, when fifty sheaves were gathered together by children. The sheaves were cleverly formed into a teepee-like structure, completely watertight inside as the rain would run off the outside sheaves, which would dry out with the sun and wind during a dry spell. Eventually, the sheaves were carried nearer the homestead to be made into a *helem* (rick or stack) which required thatching by a skilled person. It took six gambo loads to form the stack and there would be several of them on an average farm. Later on in the autumn the threshing machine, owned by a private contractor, would visit the farms to carry out the threshing, that is to separate the corn from the straw. Half the stacks were threshed in the autumn and the others kept until the spring. In the spring, each neighbour was expected to help, with his dogs, because by now the mice and rats had multiplied after spending their winter in the stacks. When the stack was dismantled to throw the sheaves into the thresher, these vermin would panic and run wild all over the place, but it never took long for some dozen or more hungry dogs to catch them all. The farmers would have made sure not to have fed the dogs that morning so that they were eager for the hunt. I heard tell that thirty vermin had shot out of one stack when it was pulled apart.

The meal at threshing time was completely different to what was provided during the hay harvest. There were not as many people involved and usually only one meal was required since the thresher was generally in a hurry to complete the work and move on to the next farm. The weather was colder and threshing took place near the farmyard so it was easier for the wife to provide a cooked meal to be eaten in the warmth of the kitchen.

I remember one farm servant, Alfred Elms, an English boy from a Barnado's home, telling us of the embarrassing behaviour of one farmer at the table after threshing. The splendid meal consisted of roast meat, two vegetables and gravy, with rice pudding to follow. The wife had put out the pudding at the same time as the main course, which gave William Evans the opportunity to transfer the rice on to his plate and mix it all up with the gravy and vegetables. Arthur had been taught proper table manners at the children's home and had been quite shocked at this spectacle. No-one said anything at the time, but there were several pairs of eyes cast in the direction of Evans y Gelli, and many a tongue wagged afterwards. Ironically enough, Evans considered himself a cut above the rest of the other farmers. On meeting a professional person, like the schoolmaster, he would choose to converse in English rather than in his native Welsh. The pity of it all was that his English was very basic and I remember him speaking at length in public, during the war, about the 'Admirality' and the enemy 'Hilter'.

Farmers and their wives had to turn their hands to all sorts of alternative enterprises in order to make both ends meet. If bills piled up it was hoped that there was a pig or calf ready for the market. My mother could recall the old practice of making butter and keeping it in earthenware crocks that held several pounds. The butter was added into it once a week and when the crock was full it was taken to a pub in town where dealers came to buy butter. They assessed the quality of the butter by boring down to the bottom of the crock, examining what they saw on the borer and paying accordingly. It was a case of take it or leave it, the poor farmer had little chance to negotiate. It was essential that the butter was the same colour and quality all through and it was that, it seems, which determined the price.

Much of a farmservant's wage was paid in food rather than cash. Living so near the sea was a blessing as it meant herring were quite cheap in season, and could be salted to keep for leaner times. Farmers had a few tricks up their sleeves in order to obtain a better price for their produce. Pigs at market were sold directly from the cart which carried them there, so presentation was of vital importance. It was soon realised that a young pig looked much larger if placed in a low-sided cart. The pigs were given a good cleaning first and if the farmer did not possess a cart with shallow sides he would borrow his neighbour's, place a thick layer of straw at the bottom and hope for the best price possible.

Emphasis is put on fresh meat now as opposed to salted bacon which was practically our sole diet of meat when I was a child, apart from the Sunday extravagance and the occasional rabbit. Killing the pig was an important annual event and most cottages had a pigsty along with the privy at the bottom of the garden. The pig would be bought as soon as it finished suckling, a small animal of about five score (100 pounds) in weight, and would be introduced to its new home in the pigsty. The pigsty was usually a stone building about eight foot square with a tiled or zinc roof and a doorway leading to an open-topped yard of smaller size with a strong door opening to the outside.

The pig was fed mainly on swill and barley meal, as well as everything that was suitable for its digestion, in order to fatten it as soon as possible. A farmer would allow his neighbours to plant a few rows of their own potatoes in his fields along with his, in exchange for help when planting and harvesting his own potatoes. The potatoes, after being allowed to dry out spread on the floor of an available building, were sorted into keepers for seed and eaters. The leftovers, which were called chats, were boiled for the pigs.

It was cheaper to buy a sow than a boar, but this could prove to be expensive. One expected to keep a pig until it grew to weigh anything up to twenty score (400 lbs). One had to be careful that it did not get too big to move through the opening to the outer yard, or to emerge through the outer door on its last day. A sow would come on heat once a month and she could be very wild and vicious at that time, so the outer door of the pigsty had to be barricaded and sometimes an all-night vigil kept when killing time was imminent. We also worried that the beast might fracture its leg due to its heavy weight and that it would be impossible to find a butcher quickly enough to kill it in time, if such a catastrophe occurred. With a sow, the date of killing was of extreme importance as it was strongly believed that the meat of a sow killed whilst on heat would not take to salting properly. For the same reason no pig should be killed when the moon was on the wane.

The day of the killing of the pig was the one of the most horrible days I had to endure as a child. This happened once a year, usually just before Christmas. It began at about six o'clock with the heating of the water. The water was heated in a cauldron, which was permanently fixed in stone and mortar along the side of the house for this yearly special event. There was room underneath for a fire, which had to be lit at this early hour so the water would be ready and boiling for the arrival of the butcher at 10 o'clock. The poor animal, whom we had loved and spoiled for the last year, was led to the slaughter and the process began by shaving the hair off its back. I cannot give the sordid details of what happened next because by now I'd be away hiding at a friend's house, some considerable distance away, until it was all over. However, the last dying squeal of the pig could be heard a few miles away, depending on the wind direction. What a relief when humane killers were introduced.

I would return for lunch, which would be fried liver with onions. The butcher used to stay for the meal, as he thought my mother cooked the ibest fried liver he had tasted. He was not so partial to any other part of the pig. The pig itself was by now hanging up against a ladder with all the internal organs removed. The butcher would return late that night, when the meat was cold, in order to cut it up. There were two rear hams, two front hams, along with two sides and the chin, all to be salted. The process of salting was rather complicated. It was carried out on a slate slab in the back kitchen (the other kitchen being the living room, the sitting room of today). Firstly, the skin was rubbed with saltpetre, followed by ordinary rock salt, until it turned into liquid with friction, then salt was put on the meat itself and dabbed into every crevice. Any veins or arteries found were cut out in case they would prevent perfect salting. The area of the hams around the bones required extra attention. After the first salting, ordinary rock salt alone was used. The salt did a great deal of harm to many houses as it seeped into the plastering, making it crumble away. To this day some of those houses where pig salting has taken place are still bothered by crumbly walls, which will not hold wallpaper, and as replastering is not always successful, they have to be lined. The richer people at the time were able to afford purchasing a *noe*, which was a watertight, deep wooden trough able to hold all the meat without it having to come in contact with any wall. Of course this big trough required room for storage which the smaller houses lacked. The meat needed daily inspection to make sure that it was all covered in salt. Every three days the old salt was cleaned off and the whole process repeated. The sides and chin were ready in ten days and were hung under the ceiling beams to dry out. The hams took three weeks of constant salting before they were ready to be hung. It was advisable to put some grease-proof paper around the base of the hanging meat lest the damp salt fall on the floor or on the head of someone passing underneath on a hot day.

All that remained of the pig was placed in a zinc bath. The lights, or lungs, and the other organs, the fry and the head had to be seen to as soon as possible, as they would not keep fresh for long without refrigeration. It was customary to present our friends and neighbours with the small joints, and they would return the compliment when they killed their pig. Possibly a refrigerator was not as essential in those days as the fire in the kitchen never gave off a great deal of heat. I can remember the thermometer which hung next to the barometer on the wall on the opposite side of the room to the fireplace reading low temperatures. We would eat as much as possible ourselves, and had the meat in some form for every meal for the next fortnight.

The fry was delicious. Today, it is called fillet and is an expensive cut. The head and trotters were soaked in salt water for a few days, washed, and then boiled for hours until all the meat came off the bones. The liquid was thrown away and having scrubbed one's hands clean, all the bones were removed, and that really meant all of them, as the smallest fragment of bone in a slice of brawn was unacceptable. All the gristle and skin was also removed and the remainder squeezed to a very messy mass. To this was added salt and pepper and some ground sage. It was all transferred into small basins, tightly packed and covered with grease-proof paper with weights applied to the surface to obtain a solid, well-sealed brawn. Often the weights would cause excess fat to ooze out around the sides of the basins. It was quite an art to make the best quality brawn, and it was well known throughout the area who could achieve this and who failed. We also melted down the two thick layers of white clean fat from the two sides into a fair quantity of lard to be solidified and stored in jars. This would provide sufficient to make pastry for quite a while.

A few women, including my mother and myself, would indulge in cleaning the intestines to make chittlings. The method of dealing with the intestines was far from pleasant but it had to be done. The small and large intestines were all placed in a large bucket and taken up the field, where there was running water. The little stream was dammed with stones so that there was a strong downward flow of water to run through these lengths of gut. The large intestine was first cut up with a large knife into lengths of about six inches and the contents squeezed out. It was then turned inside out, held under the cascading water and put in a clean bucket, the process repeated until all the large intestine was clean. It was necessary to be more careful with the narrow gut as this was used for making sausages. It was cut up into lengths of about a yard each. The contents, all liquid, were squeezed out and using a long stick the gut was turned inside out and thoroughly washed. The worse part of the job was now over. On returning to the back kitchen, the large gut was scrubbed and put to soak in brine. The stomach was cut open, also scrubbed inside and out and added to the brine. The small intestine for sausage making was put flat on a board, and with a knife, scraped to get rid of the lining, leaving the transparent skin. This was rather a delicate operation as you had to guard against piercing the skin. The meat left after trimming the hams before salting, along with any other odd bits, was minced and mixed with breadcrumbs, sage and seasoning. Filling the skins to form sausages was a laborious process and had to be done by hand as we had no modern contraption to simplify the work. Still, it was all worth it as the result was delicious. Some of the left-over meat was used for faggot making, along with minced liver, onions and breadcrumbs. It was all mixed together and separated into balls which were surrounded with cut-up pieces of the 'shawl' taken out of the pig's inside.

After several days soaked in brine it was time to wash the guts and stomach free of salt and, along with the lungs, to boil them in water for a considerable time. After allowing the mixture to cool, it was cut into small pieces, as chitterlings, and fried with bacon and onion to make a wonderful-tasting dish. The tongue remained, also to be soaked in cold water and salt, boiled and then fitted tightly into a basin, pressed down with heavy weights, allowing it to set into a nice shape when taken out of the basin.

From now on it was all joy for me. Normally the pig was killed a few days before Christmas and following that period I was usually sick and suffering from a bad tummy, having gorged myself with too much pig. I remember quite well my Aunt Sarah saying, 'If this child continues to eat meat and pickles at this rate, she will no doubt suffer with her stomach when she grows older.' What a good clairvoyant she was.

I doubt whether there are many people left who know how to salt a pig anymore. It was no mean task even after years of experience. I remember my mother who was an old hand at it, being unsuccessful on more than one occasion and several of her friends admitting defeat once in a while. The hams hanging under the beams had to be inspected often and without an extremely close scrutiny, one could hardly see if anything was wrong. Only sometimes one noticed little brownish, transparent, shed maggot skins on the floor under the hams and realised the seriousness of the situation. Down the ham would come and the source of the trouble was invariably around the big hambone. There was usually a nasty smell, the bad meat was bright red in colour and, on digging deep, the maggots would be found. It was necessary to take immediate action and cut the ham into small pieces, taking the hambone out and rescuing as much unaffected meat as possible. If not checked regularly a whole ham could be ruined. It was a sign that the meat around the bone had not been salted properly and left someone feeling very embarrassed.

On one occasion when a few farmers had gathered in the New Inn, after two of them had consumed rather a large quantity of alcohol, they started to argue about who had the best wife. Having run out of other virtues and not to be beaten, one of them announced, 'I am pretty certain that your Annie was never able to produce so many maggots in the ham as our Jane did.' When Jane heard this, it was not surprising that her husband was never again seen inside that pub or any other pub. He was made to sign the pledge to abstain from alcohol in future. The result was that he ended his days a deacon at the Methodist Church, as a result of one indiscretion!

Keeping poultry was another means of supplementing one's income. Christmas time in particular was a big occasion, when fattened birds were sold at the local Christmas Fair. *Plufio* (plucking) was an important day and neighbours would arrange among themselves not to pluck on the same day, so that they would be able to help one another in turn.

Sometimes it meant plucking all night as there were no fridges, so the work had to be done as close as possible to Fair day. Back in the thirties, one smallholding I knew of kept chickens to be killed and sold, dressed for the table, all the year round. A traveller would call every week, with an order for the following week. Their son, who was regarded as being rather simple, spent his entire time plucking chickens. As a result, he had become an expert at the job, operating very quickly without tearing any of the skin. When he went to help his neighbours at Christmas time he outclassed everyone with his speed. One farmer's wife became so concerned at the nonchalant way he was carrying on that she began to get tearful and begged Dai, 'Dai bach do be careful, for heaven's sake don't tear them or we'll never be able to sell the birds and what shall we do then?' Dai took no notice and carried on in his own sweet way with a smile on his face producing perfectly plucked birds; be it turkey, goose, duck or a chicken, Dai was the expert. Some people were far better at plucking than others, and some were so bad that they were never invited to help out again, which was a real insult.

My mother's task on all the surrounding farms was always to 'draw' the insides, and dress the bird ready for market. In later years I assisted her, after completing a course with the local Young Farmers' Club. I was pleased that it was only at Christmas time that I was called upon to exercise my new skill, as following this work, which lasted several days and nights, my hands were very swollen, with cuts deep into the skin. This was the result of tying the birds with one's hands being greasy all the time.

My mother and I had one dreadful Yuletide. It started when Cochyn (Ginger) the postman called on Christmas Day; and very nice it was too, for us but not for him. We had our duck roasting away merrily in the oven when he appeared. We expected a smile and a greeting, but quite to the contrary, he seemed most annoyed, saying that their day had been ruined, because when the wife had gone to stuff the goose on the previous day she found that the insides had not been removed. They had bought the bird from one of the farms where we had been seeing to all this. We had no defence to present. We had seen to so many birds on that farm, and anyone can make a mistake. We felt guilty enough to offer him our own duck, which was refused – as they wanted a goose or nothing at all! His next port of call was the farm in question and he was going to find out what they intended doing about the problem. We had a very miserable Christmas imagining the repercussions.

As early as possible on Boxing Day, we set off for Nant-blaen, the farm in question, to face the music, come what might. It came as a surprise when we were greeted as cordially as ever by Gwen on our arrival, as we had been steeling ourselves for accusations and reprimands. My mother came to the point at once, since there was no point in delaying the issue. 'Oh, that, what a silly fool,' was Gwen's dismissive comment. Gwen had responded to Cochyn's complaint by inviting him and his wife to join them for dinner when he had finished his round and to bring the goose with them, so that she could reimburse them. The pair never came for dinner, but turned up late that evening without the goose. When Cochyn had returned home after finishing his work, he found dinner ready. On the previous day the wife had put her hand inside the bird and had felt something there, and had left it at that. On Christmas morning after Cochyn had left the house she conducted a more thorough investigation and she found that what she thought was the goose's inside organs intact were the giblets. That is where I had been taught to put them. What a relief! We ate our Boxing Day meal with much more relish than we had our Christmas dinner!

Whilst attending elementary school, I, along with all my schoolmates, joined the Young Farmers' Club, a movement which had become very popular in the area at the time. We were taught all kind of topics associated with farming. Every Friday afternoon, Mr Powell, the County Poultry Organiser, visited the school. He held a National Diploma in Poultry, a qualification almost unheard of today. He would bring along half a dozen pullets, each in a cage, which were placed on the desks in the classroom. We were instructed how to judge them and what were the points to look for in a good bird. Each of us were given six young black Leghorn pullets on the point of laying. They had to have a shed of their own, so we cleaned out an old shed, saw that it was waterproof, put nests inside, and gave the inside a good whitewash with lime. A large run was erected outside the shed so that they could graze and be practically free range. It was a scientific project so the daily intake of food was weighed and noted, and the cost worked out. The eggs, when the pullets started to lay, were recorded and priced, in the hope of some profit at the end of the year. My birds suffered a setback at the very beginning. After a few days in the shed, they were gasping for breath, especially first thing in the morning. Poultry suffer from a disease known as gapes, which displays similar symptoms, so I started to panic. On his next visit, Mr Powell immediately realised that the thick layer of lime inside the shed was affecting their breathing. We scraped and washed down the shed walls and in no time the birds were back to normal and soon the first egg was laid.

We were also taught how to do stock judging and were then taken around the agricultural shows, large and small, to compete against other clubs in this event. A team from our club won a stock judging competition at the Olympia Dairy show one year. A member of our club represented Wales in the poultry judging competition in Ireland and I stood as reserve. We were very young teenagers at the time competing against much older competitors but it was good training for later life. Some of us were pretty ignorant as to the finer points of a cow. All I knew was that one cow could give more milk than the other and that was what was important. We were well taught in what to look for in a dairy cow. The other day I came across a pamphlet from those days, called *Stock Judging Points in a Dairy Cow*. We had to learn its contents off by heart before going to compete at a show, to understand and apply the principles as well as possible when trying to place four cows in the correct order of merit. In the larger shows we would have to outline the reasons for our decisions over the microphone.

Stock Judging Points – Dairy Cow

1   HEAD – feminine in character, long and
          finely cut.

>   a) horns – curving slightly inwards and
>   of nice quality, small in size.
>
>   b) forehead – broad, eyes large and
>   prominent, of gentle expression.
>
>   c) nostrils – wide and expansive.
>
>   d) nose – clean, no darkness.

2   NECK – lean but not weak.

3   WITHERS – not too wide.

4   SHOULDERS – flat and sloping.

5   CHEST – broad and deep, not running light at girth.

6   BARREL – deep with well-sprung ribs.

7   BACK – broad over loins and coming to a point
          at the shoulder, forming a wedge shape,
          the top line to be straight from tail to
          withers.

8   HIPS – wide apart and light in bone.

9   RUMP – long, broad and level with tail, fine and
          neatly set in.

10   HIND QUARTERS – wide not too fleshy.

11 UDDER – well-carried, not hanging loose and swinging (not pendulous), thin-skinned, not fleshy and not split up between quarters. Udder should extend well forward in a line with the belly extending high up towards the tail end (avoid pocket in hind bag).

    a) teats – of good, even size and quality, squarely placed and wide apart (avoid bottle teats).

    b) Milk veins – tortuous and plain.

12 SKIN – thin, mellow and flexible to the touch.

13 FLESH – level and even, not showing any signs of beef on any part.

14 CARRIAGE AND ACTION IN WALKING – smart and gay-looking.

15 GENERAL APPEARANCE – symmetrical, combining size with scope.

Percentage of Maximum marks suggested for these points:

Head and neck	10
Shoulders	10
Back, loins and ribs	20
Hindquarters and tail setting	10
Udder, teats and milk veins	30
General appearance viz. –	
type, size, colour, bloom, etc.	20
Total	100

This was before the modern practice of dehorning calves.

Despite all this experience and being country born and bred I have to confess to some fear of certain animals. From an early age I was terrified of horses and shire-horses in particular. I lived next door to *yr efail* (the smithy) and spent my childhood days playing with the blacksmith's grandson, Dai'r Efail. When one of these giants came to be shod we were given the choice of leaving or staying inside the smithy until the work was done. Once having made that decision there was no turning back as the large doors were kept closed throughout. I still marvel to think of the enormous size of these shire-horses when confined in an enclosed building which they practically filled. Dai and I operated the bellows, one either side of the fire, blowing it up to maintain the heat. The blacksmith placed the horseshoe in the fire using long tongs, until it was red hot so he could hammer it into shape on the anvil, then he immersed it in cold water, held in a small trough. This made a loud sizzling noise and steam filled the place. The belief was that this water could cure warts and sufferers used to bring their bottles to the smithy to fill. While Dai and I were temporary prisoners in the smithy we were supplied with sandwiches filled with Demerara. These we toasted on a long fork over the fire until the butter and sugar melted, creating a mouth-watering delicacy.

Outside the smithy was the *plat bando* (a hooping plate), a large, circular plate about an inch in thickness with a big, round hole cut out of the centre and fixed to the ground about a foot off the floor. The day for fitting the iron rim on the wooden wheels of carts was a notable event. The wheelwright who had made the wooden wheels, along with the owner and a few helpers, would turn up at the smithy with the wheels. The blacksmith had a selection of iron bands of varying sizes from which to choose. The wheel was placed on the hooping plate, the band put in the fire to expand until red then rushed out to be hammered on to the wheel. At this point, buckets full of water were poured over the wheel to cool it quickly, to prevent the wood from burning and to contract the metal tightly on to the wheel. Speed was imperative in this process and there was no time to waste on pleasantries; indeed the odd swear word was not infrequently heard when it was felt that someone was not moving with sufficient urgency. Yet, after a good meal at the end of the day, any tension was quickly resolved. At other times, during the fine weather, we would have picnics on the *plat bando* and it served as a table for birthday celebrations. After the blacksmith died in his eighties his family sold the contents of the smithy, mainly for scrap. I regret to this day not having taken the opportunity to buy the hooping plate and the anvil as they were associated with some happy memories of days long ago.

The blacksmith was a big strong man who always wore a thick, woollen vest and a flannel shirt made locally from flannel weaved at the nearby woollen mills. They produced red flannel, bands of which were worn inside vests by sufferers of rheumatism and chest complaints, also those with back problems. It is some years now since we had a visitor here from England, who bought himself some red flannel material in order to have two body belts made. Not so long ago I heard from the same gentleman, who wanted me to buy some more red flannel material for him as the old belts were worn out. It is no mean task to find red flannel these days as it does not seem to be woven in the area any more. However, with the help of family and friends I managed to find him some.

I found life difficult with my fear of large horses as I used to walk through fields to visit a neighbouring farm and happily grazing in one was Captain the shire-horse. He was a lovely-looking animal and supposed to be very docile, but I was terrified of him. I had met him before when he was being shod in the smithy – he was none too gentle then. I hurried through the field, keeping my eyes looking towards the hedge and away from Captain, hoping that he would not see me.

Crossing the next field was even more frightening. At the bottom of this field was another farm and they kept a very ill-tempered greyhound. He seemed to have an uncanny ability to sense the presence of someone crossing the top end of the field to Ffynnon-oer. On becoming aware of an intruder, he would race across the field to meet them barking and showing his teeth, and he was not unknown, if annoyed, to take a bite out of his victim's leg. My only solution was to creep along as quietly as possible, keeping my eyes averted from the farm, praying fervently all the while.

The farm next door kept geese and turkeys, to be fattened for Christmas. The turkeys grew to be huge birds and they chased anyone who dared set foot on the farmyard, gobbling away, spreading their wings and displaying a show of great annoyance. There was a pond outside the farm entrance and the geese enjoyed their daily bath in it. If anyone happened to pass during their exercise, the gander would immediately notice a stranger and start to give chase. I learnt how to deal with this bird: as soon as he started to hiss and chase I would catch hold of the big brute by his neck and drag him along with me. He did not like this treatment and he would soon give up the fight and return to his harem in the water.

But these hazards were nothing compared to my absolute horror of rats, which has never left me. These creatures seemed to have plagued my early years. My first real encounter with rats involved the outside toilet, when I was about eight years old. When I was compelled to go visiting in the night, there was no light at the touch of a switch to guide us on our way, as the luxury of electricity was unheard of and would be for almost the next twenty years. It was a question of either making use of a torch or going in the dark. We loved moonlight nights. I had by now journeyed so often to the little house down the bottom of the garden that I knew the way blindfolded. One night, when it was very dark and stormy, carrying an unlit torch, having closed the door and sat on the seat, I heard a very faint noise and then felt something furry touching my leg. I switched on the torch and there was a huge rat facing me. As I had closed the door there was no way out for it. I jumped onto the seat, miraculously avoiding falling into the hole. It was impossible to reach the door latch from the position I was in, but there was no alternative but to remain in that position, praying that the rat would not climb up onto the seat. I held my torch very tightly in my hand ready to defend myself if need be. Eventually someone in the house realised that I'd been away a long time so thankfully a rescue party came to find out. Whenever I mention this tale to my husband he thinks he can improve on it by reminding me of the time a rat went up the inside of his trouser leg when in the RAF in Sri Lanka during the last war. He is none the worse for his experience, but never goes near rats without wellies or trousers in socks.

Another encounter occurred when my mother went to feed the chickens with feed kept in an old milk churn in the barn. Luckily for her she saw the rat before putting her hand and the small saucepan inside the churn. The rat had to be killed. My mother found a pitchfork and kept stabbing at it, whilst I, on being called to help, and not daring to show my real fear, had to stand close by holding a fork, making certain that it would not escape. It tried very hard, fighting for its life. It was a horrid encounter but we won and managed to kill it in the end. Survival was the name of the game in those days.

During the Second World War, the rat population was such a problem that the Local Authority decided to recruit a 'rat catcher'. The services of this person were given free to householders but farmers and smallholders had to pay a fee. Business people also seemed to be exempt or at least some of them were able to get away with not paying. By now the rats were almost taking over our outbuildings, attracted by the cattle food, which the blacksmith next door sold as a sideline. When he was forced to call in the rat catcher, the officer's expert opinion was that it was no use putting bait down on the smithy side without doing the same on our side. Fair play to him, he thought it only right that the operation should be carried out on the two premises at the same time, and that no payment should be expected from us. We consented to this after several reassurances from the catcher that the bait was harmless to all other animals, including pigs. The work was carried out meticulously, with the bait placed inside lengths of piping and hidden away from domestic animals, making it all extremely safe.

At this time our pig, Sue, was almost ready for the gallows and despite the care taken by the rat catcher, my mother was still concerned for her safety. Feeling very ill at ease she ventured out the following night armed with the hurricane lamp, to see if Sue was all right. In no time at all she was back calling for help, and as I approached the pigsty I could hear loud, crunching noises. However much I feared rats, quick action was necessary. My mother had a fork in her hand and gave me a big stick. By the light of the lamp we could see rats everywhere in the yard of the pigsty, some looked dead, others half dead, moving about very slowly. Sue had gone absolutely mad and was doing her best to eat them. My mother was desperate for the pig to be saved, she was too valuable to be lost at this stage. We had no idea how much poison her system could withstand and it was better to be safe than sorry. I was ordered to hold the lamp with one hand and with the other to hit poor Sue's snout with the stick hard enough for her to let go of the rat in her mouth, and to stop her picking up more. My mother removed the rats out of the pigsty as quickly as possible. I have never forgotten the experience. We won the battle and Sue was none the worse for her ordeal. Sows are known to eat their offspring and to eat swill, which is a varied mixture, as part of their diet. It proves pigs to be omnivores. With the constant new regulations confronting the farmer, pigs are no longer allowed to enjoy swill.

This was not the last of my problems with rats. I studied Zoology as one of the subjects for my Higher School Certificate, which of course meant studying certain animals and insects and having to dissect them in class. The list included a rat, a dogfish, a crayfish, a cockroach and an earthworm. Specimens were difficult to obtain as it was wartime. There were plenty of rats and earthworms available but no-one wanted to catch a rat, so as a rabbit had a similar anatomy, a rabbit it was every time. I enjoyed the subject but declared at the start that if the visiting examiner brought a rat for dissection in the exam it would be impossible for me to answer that part of the exam. I lived in hope until the much-dreaded day dawned, when the examiner visited the school to examine the three of us in the practical work, bringing his own undisclosed specimen with him. When he entered the laboratory we were ready and in position. He carried a large travelling case which looked as if it was going to burst any minute. I held my breath while he lifted it onto the teacher's bench and started to open it, with our teacher, Mrs Hughes, standing behind him ready to peep at the contents. On his lifting the lid and seeing the object to be dissected, she shot one glance across the room at me and I immediately knew, yes, it was a rat. There was a threat in her eyes, followed by a pleading look. She was not allowed to speak to us, but, outside the window there was a man on a ladder. She found this an excuse to come over to find out if his presence disturbed me in any way. All she said was, 'You dare. Get on with it.' I took a few minutes to debate with myself and then realised that I had been brave enough on that awful night to help save a pig's life, surely passing my exam was as important to me.

So my Cardi survival kit came into action. The rat I was given was a white one, pickled, looking very much the worse for wear and smelling very strongly of formalin. It had been to another school before visiting us and its digestive system had already been removed. Our task involved exposing the thoracic cavity, to find the heart and isolate the arteries, veins and nerves leading to and from it. This was virtually an impossible task as the rat was almost in a state of decay and too brittle to make any sense out of the exam question. It was the same for the three of us as we each had a rat in the same condition. One could only try one's best and use one's memory to draw as good a picture of what one had done as one could under the circumstances. It was unfortunate that one had to dissect the upper part of the body so close to the head, as this was the part I found most objectionable. I managed it all by fooling myself that I was dealing with a small rabbit. The Botany practical examination was quite as bad, being confronted with old and wilted specimens. No student today would put up with this kind of treatment and although the teachers complained nothing happened.

Years later whilst working at a medical research establishment in England I came across the old rat again. They were bred for experimental purposes, to research human diseases, so at the end of the day the rat has proved itself useful to us. I rarely see one now – save the occasional one at our compost heap at the bottom of the garden – so I know they are still around.

Cats have always played their part in keeping the rodent population down. Unfortunately they can have the unfortunate habit of displaying their kill and I witnessed one of our cats dragging a big rat into the house. Was she expecting praise from us for her initiative or did she think we were short of food so she was prepared to share her feast with us?

Cats have strange ways of behaving. All farm cats are generally kept outside to keep a check on rats and mice, so they don't get fed. They snuggle in between the hay and straw bales and they look so comfortable that one can envy them at times. After a visit from a strange Tom, one can expect the arrival of a number of kittens in a few weeks time. Cats are such cunning animals and know better than to trust humans so they develop a sixth sense and always hide their young in all kind of unexpected places. Farmers could be very cruel, or perhaps they were only being practical as the cat population had to be culled at times. This was usually done by drowning kittens as soon as possible after birth. Once the kittens were old enough to open their eyes and look as appealing as kittens can, it required a very hard-hearted farmer to drown them. A nearby farm, situated close to rows of houses, has a very wily feline who is fully aware that the occupants of these houses love cats. She manages to hide her kittens whilst very young and as soon as she thinks they are old enough she carries them one by one in her mouth across the fields to show the neighbours, showing off her offspring. Who can resist such a beautiful ball of fluff? In this way she can assure them of a good home. Some of these when grown to full size sometimes visit the farm looking like overfed monsters in comparison to the leaner farm cats.

I believe that there are domesticated cats and wild ones. It is the domesticated one who by some misfortune has landed as a farm cat, that sees to it that her offspring enjoy a better life than hers, having to hunt for her food. To the wild cat this is a way of life and she enjoys it. Although she may not refuse food from humans, she will resist any friendship and on no account will she be touched. She trains her young to hunt at an early age, to be self-sufficient and to refrain from being mollycoddled by humans. Domestic cats are easily house trained whilst the wild ones will never go near a cat litter tray.

Chapter 5

~ Upstairs and Downstairs ~

Let not Ambition mock their useful Toil
Their homely Joys and Destiny obscure;
Nor Grandeur hear with a disdainful smile,
The short and simple Annals of the Poor.

Thomas Gray,
'An Elegy written in a Country Churchyard'

The village life of Blaen-y-groes was dominated by a typical mansion built by the gentry, employing several of the local people as staff. The old lady of the house lived to be ninety years of age and, according to my mother, had very little faith in fresh air. She was always wrapped up, no window was allowed open and any draught was to be avoided at all cost. The Colonel fought in the Boer War, at the end of which the entire village gathered to celebrate his safe home-coming. Hung across the entrance of the mansion was a banner with the words 'Welcome Home, Colonel', which my grandmother had painstakingly cut out from remnants of material and sewn on a sheet.

The old Colonel drank himself to death, the result perhaps of his war experience. Like most mansions of its kind in the area, the place had to be sold in 1925 to cover death duties, with the occupants having to move to more modest homes and lead more modest lives. Glanaber never reverted to its former glory. It remained empty for seven years and after two farming owners occupied it for twenty-five years it was converted to a hotel. Later it was taken over by a community of people running it as a co-operative unit. It is sad to see the old stone entrance with its solid, heavy, wrought-iron gates and the rhododendron drive, now in a state of decay, with only the memory of its former glory remaining.

The family's coach was a familiar sight in the village and local youngsters would vie with each other to open the mansion gates when they heard the coach coming down the drive. Since they were always rewarded for their trouble, it was common practice to close the great wrought-iron gates when the horses were heard approaching, in order to claim their remuneration for ostentatiously opening them again. By some miraculous instinct, there was always somebody near enough to hear the coach on its way.

The family had a very strict spinster as housekeeper. As my grandmother had been well educated, she was one of the few in the village who could speak fluent English at that time. Because of this, Miss Ady took it upon herself to visit our home on her weekly half-day off. This was not unrewarded, since as a repayment for a visit and afternoon tea, she would send the gardener to prune the fruit trees in the orchard and do anything else that required professional treatment in the garden, bringing with him some plants and cuttings. As a result we had one of the best gardens in the village. It was not beyond the lady of the mansion herself to pay my grandmother a visit. On one occasion whilst the coach was travelling along the main road, one of the horses bolted. The lady was thrown out without receiving serious injury. Although there were other houses nearer to the scene of the accident, she insisted on being carried to Granny's house, to wait the arrival of the doctor, which would take a long time in those days.

The lady's maid, Maud Hughes, was an extraordinarily kind person who was made to pay heavily for her generosity. There was considerable poverty in the area and a great deal of illness. Miss Hughes stole from the mansion, mostly bedclothes and essentials that were required by the needy and sick. She seemed to have cast herself in the role of a latter-day Robin Hood. Yet it was the recipients of her kindness who betrayed her to her employers. As a result she was immediately dismissed from her post and was told never to look for a similar position in this country, as they would refuse to give her a character reference.

She was an extremely smart young woman and the son of one of the local farms was sweet on her. It was rumoured later that she had given jewellery from the mansion to this man's sisters in order to gain popularity by his family, but still they did not approve of her as they considered her to be working class. They wanted him to marry the dowdy daughter of a local farmer, for whom he felt no affection whatsoever. In the end neither got him as he fell ill with what today I am sure would have been diagnosed as cancer of the spine. Poor man, he suffered terribly with none of today's modern drugs available. He was nursed at home and the stolen bedclothes became very useful. After he died, his sisters showed their appreciation, or surely lack of it, by buying a black hat for the farmer's daughter to wear at the funeral and nothing for the girl for whom he truly cared. Maud Hughes, through loyal friends, managed to find a post in Scotland and she spent the remainder of her working days there. Although my family were very friendly with her, thankfully no Glanaber property found its way to our house. After she was denounced as a thief my mother and aunt were amongst the few who stood by her, whilst others, who had profited from her generosity deserted her. She always remembered this and sent me a Christmas present every year until I'd left childhood behind. She eventually returned to her native land to enjoy retirement, along with her sister, who had been a cook in one of the royal households. I was privileged to be invited to her funeral along with another lady whose family had remained friendly with her in her hour of need. It was a very sad, poignant occasion, although I myself was too young to remember her having to leave Glanaber.

It always puzzled me that my Aunt Nell had remained unmarried all her life, despite her reputation as a great beauty in her youth. A contemporary of hers who was something of a Casanova in his heyday used to tease me, saying, 'You are quite a nice girl, but what a pity that you are nowhere near as pretty as your Aunt Nell.'

I only recently learned the sad but romantic tale of Aunt Nell's courtship. I had heard of her many admirers and one day whilst making a thorough search of the *cwtsh dan star* (cupboard under the stairs) I found dozens of old picture postcards, sent to my family by relatives and friends. A good many of them had been sent from different parts of America when my uncles were working there. As there were no rural telephones in the early twentieth century a postcard, invariably a picture one, was the best means of communication. At that time a postcard was much cheaper to send than a letter, and the post seemed to be more reliable than it is today. In an emergency, when neither letter nor card would do, somebody who owned a horse would be willing to help by fetching a doctor.

Of course, as a result of all this information relayed on cards, the postman knew all the details of the lives of the villagers, their friends and relations. It was said that a certain inquisitive farmer's wife provided the postman with a hearty meal of ham and eggs in return for being allowed to have a quick glance at what was inside the postbag as he devoured his breakfast. Cochyn the postman would approach the door of a house and shout out the information before anyone had chance to see the card. His method of giving out news resembled a town crier. 'Your Jim is in Fishguard. He will catch a train for London and will arrive home at the end of the week. Here's the card.' (One cannot but notice that Uncle Jim, arriving from America, after docking in Fishguard, some twenty odd miles from home, seemed to have to travel all the way to London in order to come home.) When the postcards contained rather personal and intimate information, drastic measures had to be taken to fool Cochyn. A few clever and resourceful individuals did manage to master writing in reverse so that the contents could only be read when held up to a mirror.

Amongst these postcards were some that revealed the identity of my Aunt's true love, a poet called Jack. They also told the story of their tragic love affair that lasted for twelve years. Jack came from a nearby village and had obviously taken a fancy to Nell, as had many other lads in the district. His education had, perforce, been basic, but he and Nell corresponded in perfect English. He was very gifted, but poverty forced him to take a position as an apprentice grocer in Aberdare, far from home and Nell. He communicated with her constantly, often through romantic verses on postcards. The frequent letters that must have passed between them, which doubtless contained more information, must have been destroyed, but the story can still be pieced together. While Jack remained in south Wales, Nell of course went to London to join her brother Griff, who had a milk business in the city.

Jack and Nell made sure that their visits home coincided so that they could still meet from time to time, but the majority of their courting took place by post. Despite his lack of opportunity, Jack was highly ambitious. He saved up in the hope of gaining an education and immersed himself in cultural activities, gaining a reputation as no mean poet. He achieved his ambition when he entered the University College at Cardiff, where he won the chair at the College Eisteddfod for his poetry. In 1912 he entered the Theological College at Carmarthen with the intention of becoming a Congregationalist minister. During his period at Cardiff his courtship with Nell seemed to have cooled somewhat and one of the postcards he wrote indicated that he had proposed marriage and had been rejected. I did hear that one of the problems was that Nell was a few inches taller than Jack – this appeared to be a major problem at the time. Poor Griffith Beynon the Minister at Capel Seion had been rejected for the same reason as we have heard. Whatever caused the rift there was still occasional communication, but Jack's missives were now signed 'Best wishes, Jack' rather than the previous 'All my love' or 'Forever Yours'. Perhaps the strain of being apart for so long was beginning to show. However after Jack returned to Carmarthen the relationship regained its old fervour and a happy ending seemed to be in sight. It was then, after all the years of courtship, that tragedy struck.

In August of 1916 Jack attended a YMCA conference in Brecon. One boiling hot day he and a group of friends went for a swim in the river to cool off. Although he was normally a strong swimmer, Jack drowned. The romantic hopes expressed in his poems to Nell were never fulfilled. Nell, who had remained faithful to him for so many years as he strove to make his way in the world, was heartbroken. Although other suitors came calling, she remained faithful to the memory of her poet and, after years of ill health, she died before reaching the age of sixty. I have found the most romantic poem written by Jack to Nell, in her autograph album, in the month of May prior to his death in August. It always bring tears to my eyes whenever I read it. Life can be very cruel at times.

Rhywun

Na'i thonnog wallt nid ydyw'r nos
Yng nghoed y cwm yn dduach,
Na gwawr ei llygaid Gwener dlos
Erioed ni fu'n ddisgleiriach,
Yn hud ei gwên mae serch bob dydd
Yn mynnu sôn am 'Ellen',

A hon yw'r ddofn gyfrinach gudd –
Fy nef yw cwmni Rhywun.

Caiff pendefigion byd eu hedd
Mewn gwanc am aur a thiroedd,
Yn sawr y cwpan gwin a'r medd
Mae mwyniant i frenhinoedd,
I Fardd fy Ngwlad ar lwybrau Mai
Mae'r gwir ddedwyddwch cyfrin,
Caf finnau wynfyd sy'n ddi-drai,
A Nef yng nghwmni Rhywun.

Jack

The translation of such passion is difficult; one can only hope that Casi Dylan's following attempt comes close to the original:

Someone

Darker than the wooded vale
At night is my love's hair,
Her Venus eyes that sweetly shine
Are bright beyond compare.
The magic of her loving smile
Insists on tales of Helen
Deep in me is secret joy –
My heaven shared with Someone.

The princes of this world may quest
For might in gold and manor,
Kings are provided well enough
With finest wines and porter.
On May-time walks a poet finds

His joy and inspiration.
I find eternal paradise
In Heaven, shared with Someone.

Jack

The social life of Blaen-y-groes revolved around the school, where most gatherings were held during the evenings, when people were not attending chapel meetings. The Cardis loved committees, be it Parish, Hall, or Bull Society. There was a Ploughing Match Committee as well and it is known that a Ploughing Match was held in the village as far back as 1878, when the school was closed for the day. On that occasion, the champion ploughman came from another village some ten miles away. The contestants must have been very skilled considering that they were not able to bring their own horses, because of the distance involved, so had to borrow them from local farmers. There was always a Novice class and there were also competitions for building and trimming hedges.

The Local Authority also held classes at the school, one of the most popular being the carpentry class. Glanaber was also a venue for classes conducted in one of their elegant outhouses. Buttermaking classes were held with an instructress coming from north of the county. Some of the students were rather sceptical about the value of these classes and felt they made better butter at home, without the benefit of instruction. My mother always maintained that her home-made butter never contained the white streaks that appeared in the well-decorated butter brought home from class.

Since time immemorial it seems the seaside village of

Aber-porth, some miles from Blaen-y-groes, has celebrated *Dydd Iau Mawr* each year on the second Thursday in August, followed by *Dydd Iau Bach* on the following Thursday. These two days were regarded as a holiday for the farmers between two harvests, after the hay harvest and before the corn harvest. *Dydd Iau Mawr* was meant for the farmers and *Dydd Iau Bach* for their servants. It has been suggested that this practice originated with a religious festival dating back to the Middle Ages. It has been said that in one year, at the end of the 1920s, as many as eight thousand people descended on Aber-porth on the second Thursday in August.

They came from several miles around, in their horse-drawn traps and carts, and it could be very difficult to find room for all the vehicles and a place to leave the horses. The seaside ladies used to prepare teas to sell on those days and local women were engaged to help. Some of the visitors would bring their own food and only buy boiling water for making tea. Only a few would be brave enough to discard their clothes and enter the water, although most were prepared to paddle, the ladies lifting their long skirts. Others were daring enough to tuck their skirts inside their knickers to have more freedom of movement. The men took their socks off and rolled up their trousers but still kept their caps on. The ones who entered the sea were usually teased unmercifully that they only did so because this was the one time during the year when they took their clothes off to have a bath. The sea water was considered a great healer for many complaints, and this yearly treatment for the feet was supposed to work wonders. Some used to bring buckets to take home filled with sea water, although one wonders how much of it was left after the rough journey home in the carts. Sea water was also regarded as a disinfectant which cleansed anything poured into it, as sea pollution was unheard of in those days.

There was entertainment as well, carnival and sports during the day and a concert during the evening. After the last war there was less enthusiasm for the two Thursdays and the horse-drawn vehicles were replaced by coaches and cars. The entertainment now included cricket matches as well as pony rides. The decline continued as the beaches increasingly became the focus for summer visitors to the seaside villages.

The chapels also had their Sunday School summer outings to the nearest beach. The members (not just the faithful ones!) and children would turn up in horse-drawn carts and gambos belonging to the farmers of the chapel. The ladies would bring their baskets laden with an abundance of food. Catering for the masses was made easier thanks to the assistance of one member of Capel Seion, who lived close to Aber-porth beach. She provided vast quantities of boiling water for the gallons of tea required to slake the thirst of the visitors. Welsh wives never organised these meals beforehand. Instead they would all turn up with their baskets full and by some mysterious intuition always seemed to get the right balance between the cakes and the savouries. There was no organised form of entertainment either, apart from sports for the children. Very few of the chapel's children and adults would venture near the water as they could not afford to get their best clothes wet and dirty, so it was best behaviour throughout the day. If it rained there was a vestry quite close to the beach which belonged to a small chapel, a branch of Capel Seion, so that everyone could go inside out of the wet. The men enjoyed themselves sitting around, relaxing, discussing their problems and exchanging views. The ladies, as usual, spent most of their day preparing food, so it was hardly a holiday for them. There were two meals to be served, followed by the clearing up, all of which was left entirely to the women as men in those days were not expected to involve themselves in domestic chores.

With so many changes in society, it is perhaps not surprising that such lavish feasts are becoming less common. In the chapels, however, the old methods prevail, to the great satisfaction of all involved. It was recently decided that when the Ladies Missionary Society meet in various chapels that the tea afterwards should be confined to Welsh cakes and buns to avoid competition between chapels. This lasted for a few sessions, but one chapel broke the rule and everyone was pleased to follow suit, and were soon back to the wonderful tea parties of old. Several types of sandwiches, sausage rolls, fruit cake, *bara brith*, Welsh cakes, sponges of all description, brown and white bread, butter and cheese were all on the menu once again. It is worth seeing the fifty or so local Methodist deacons at the close of their Presbytery meeting, tucking in with gusto to plates full of salad, followed by trifle and a wide assortment of mouth-watering cakes, all prepared for free by the ladies of the chapel where the meeting was held.

Having left Blaen-y-groes for a while to pursue a university education and a period working at a research establishment in England, I returned secure in the belief that there was not much left to learn. I soon found that I had been gravely mistaken, for six months of running a chapel Sale of Work taught me more about human nature than the best college in the land.

The saga began when Capel Seion required funds to decorate its buildings. It was unanimously agreed to hold a Sale of Work in the spring and to prepare for it during the autumn and winter months. We were to meet once a week in the vestry on a Tuesday night and all the female villagers, members or not, were welcomed to join us. Of course we did not expect any men to turn up, although some did, including the minister and the deacons. It all started off very well; a respectable gathering turned up on the first night and it went from strength to strength. But the minister, the Reverend Abel Price, was none too pleased with the turn out, as he was still holding a prayer meeting one night a week, at which he would be lucky to find about a dozen of the faithful attending. Our argument in response was that whilst people were attending our meetings they were safe inside the four walls of the vestry, with him in command, and that we could commence the weekly gathering with a prayer, if he so wished, hence no evil would possess their souls during those few hours. I do not think that he completely agreed with our reasoning but decided to call a truce and to accept that there was nothing wrong with our social gathering, held to raise funds to decorate our chapel.

The Welsh people would describe our minister on the whole as being a 'worldly man'. When we wanted to hold a raffle to swell the coffers of the decorating fund, which was unacceptable according to the rules and regulations of the

Presbyterian Church, he turned up trumps; provided we sold no tickets inside the holy buildings, it was all right by him. We never considered the lobby as being 'inside', so if we wanted to sell raffle tickets during the meeting, we would go out to the lobby to carry out our transactions there. This meant that the organiser of the raffle spent the best part of the evening lurking in the lobby, conducting illicit dealings with a constant stream of customers. It would have appeared highly suspicious to any stranger who had turned up for the evening to see groups of two or three people constantly traipsing off to the lobby for no apparent reason.

As part of our preparations for the sale, it was decided to invest in a large quantity of wool and some material to give to the ladies to produce knitted and sewn garments to sell at the sale. Luckily for us, the husband of one of the members was the manager of a local woollen factory, so we were able to get the wool from him at a reasonable price.

At this time a retired English lady, Mrs Dickens, who was very fond of knitting, lived in the village. She volunteered to knit ladies hats, all from one pattern, and was prepared to knit to order, as long as we provided the wool. I can still picture those caps to this day: a sort of ordinary skull cap with the brim turned back and part of the cap also turned back from the crown, so it looked like a mushroom over the head. There was no doubt that it was a very distinctive pattern, issued by the well-known wool manufacturers Patons and Baldwin, and the caps soon acquired a degree of fame in the neighbourhood. There were four colours to choose from and in a very short time almost every woman – some fifty in all – at the meetings wore one. But it did not end there: aunties, mothers, grannies, sisters, sisters-in-law, cousins and distant relatives all had caps. In fact you could not go anywhere without seeing someone wearing one. It almost amounted to an epidemic. It was, of course, good news for us and ensured that the money kept pouring into the coffers.

However, despite the success of this venture, we did have one or two upsets, for we still had the two sisters, Kitty and Lily, to contend with. One was quite wealthy and gave the impression of being frail, whilst the other was a healthy, strong woman who mothered her sister. As they had proved in the past, they could at times be very difficult, as only dear old ladies can.

I often lost patience with them. Their parents at one time had lived in the Rhondda, quite close to my Uncle Tom. Their father was a good man, but the mother had taken to drinking rather heavily, which left the family short of money and Uncle Tom lent them a considerable sum to pay their large outstanding debts. In those days there were no paper transactions amongst friends, one was simply expected to repay debts as soon as one could. Although life improved for this gentleman, especially after the death of his wife, the debt was never repaid. My uncle never missed the money, but other members of the family, including ourselves, could have done with it. I often felt very annoyed with the sisters' selfish behaviour. I have no idea whether they knew about the debt, but it would have been more than my life's worth to have mentioned it to anyone, in case it came back to their ears.

In the middle of the production of the caps, they approached me saying that they were not too happy with the quality or the colour of the wool. It was Welsh wool and perhaps slightly rough, but cheap and plentiful. All the other women seemed perfectly happy with their caps and wore them with pride.

'We are sure you won't mind, but we have already bought our own wool and given it to Mrs Dickens. She was a little worried that you wouldn't approve, but we told her it was quite all right, as we'll be giving all the money to the funds.'

I am sure that Mrs Dickens was wise to their little tricks and had insisted that they discussed their latest venture with me and the treasurer before starting with the knitting. All this did not go down well with the other members and quite a lot of persuasion and tact had to be applied to return the house to order.

By this stage of the proceedings the bulk of the work was being carried out by people in their own homes and the regular Tuesday night meeting had become nothing more than a social gathering, although a few still pretended to click their knitting needles. Each meeting ended with a cup of tea. It all started quite modestly with a cup of tea and a Welsh cake, with a nominal charge paid into the kitty. Two pairs of ladies volunteered in turn to be responsible each evening for providing the tea. After two meetings, a third pair came and asked whether they could provide sandwiches as well as Welsh cakes. Not having given it much thought, the treasurer and I answered, 'Why not, it will increase the takings.' Ham sandwiches proved very popular with all and sundry and on the next Tuesday we had sandwiches and a cake. The following week we were provided with two types of sandwiches, ham and salmon, plus a selection of small cakes. This led to more types of sandwiches and more variety of cakes being provided in subsequent weeks. In the end we had enough food to sell some at the end of every meeting, with women buying enough to fill their husband's sandwich box for work the following day and for their children's tea. We were in business!

I had never before belonged to this highly competitive world, but my mother had. Although in her seventies, she was not to be beaten when it came to my turn to provide the food, along with my friend Winnie. It was decided to make one cherry cake and one Madeira cake, since this combination had never been offered before. No expense was spared in the pursuit of perfection. The first effort with the cherry cake was a complete disaster: it sank in the centre and was soggy. The second attempt was not much better as all the cherries sank to the bottom. It was every cook's nightmare. Give in? No way! As the saying goes, three tries for a Welshman and woman and we were eventually successful. The Madeira cake gave very little trouble and our large selection of little cakes proved to be a great success. At home we were eating portions of cherry cake for some time. The cakes had to be fairly large ones to provide for all the customers, so the ironmongers in the area were doing well, since many of the housewives had to buy new cake tins.

Things went from bad to worse and entertainment was now being suggested for these evenings. We agreed that the person in charge of the evening's food could, if they chose, arrange a show at their own expense, on condition that we would be informed of the programme in advance. It all worked well and we had a show of holiday slides, a record player playing Welsh tunes and an occasional local artist, until it was the turn of those two dear sisters, Kitty and Lily, to provide the entertainment for the evening. They had arranged well in advance for somebody to show slides. But, true to form, they turned up on my doorstep, wreathed in sweet smiles, hoping that I would not be annoyed with them, and who could when they were always so full of good intentions? It was only occasionally that I felt tempted to wring their necks. They had cancelled the person they had already engaged to show slides, so they had given him a 'little something' as compensation. Instead they had engaged a professional trio to entertain us. I was not to worry about anything as they had it all in hand. This was obviously an attempt to go one better than all the other ladies, and one that the committee would never had agreed to had they been informed beforehand. Kitty and Lily obviously saw their opportunity to triumph over their neighbours with this display of generosity, by presenting us with a *fait accompli*. More trouble again, more explanations and more apologies, having to beg ladies not to stay away from an evening that, despite everything, turned out to be a huge success.

One evening we had a Bring and Buy sale at which dear Kitty and Lily were once again at their best. They decided that they could help best by pricing some of the items for sale. My tarts, for some strange reason only known to them, were worth far less than smaller ones made by a close friend of theirs. Also, all the eggs brought were free range, laid by hens grazing in the fields and very much the same size, but they did not price them equally. The wife of the senior deacon, according to them, had far better eggs than anybody else, although to the onlooker and customers they looked no different from the others. However, they were able to sell some of these top-quality eggs and I heard them telling people, 'These are Mrs Richards' eggs, so much nicer than the others.' Some people can be fooled by this type of talk, no doubt. I made no bones about my tarts, but some farmers' wives did create about the pricing of the eggs. The two dears were very upset that anyone could dare to suggest that they had done anything unfair. But then they probably considered writing malicious anonymous letters to be a perfectly innocent pastime!

It reminds me of another story involving the ladies. Their friend, Bessie Llewelyn, the lady who had baked the superior tarts, used to give them a bottle of sherry for Christmas. I called one day at their house and was offered a glass, which I declined as I did not drink alcohol. They assured me that they also were teetotal but as Bessie had given them the bottle, they felt it right for them to offer drinks to others. They now felt very guilty about this and asked my advice as to whether they were doing anything wrong in offering drinks to chapel members. After all their indiscretions, I doubt whether one extra would make any difference!

We were fortunate enough in having some teenagers turn up every week and on the evening of our last meeting we had a grand finale with a bachelor's evening when four boys took over the catering. Wonderful as they had been, the spreads that we had previously enjoyed were nothing to compare with the feast provided by these boys. We saw mothers inside the vestry who had not been seen there for years and they had worked harder in making their sons' evening a success than they would have done for themselves. It all ended with a good Welsh singsong.

The day of the sale dawned and we were all ready, extremely happy with the proceeds up to this stage. There were a number of stalls set up, including a jumble stall with sack-loads of items. Needless to say we made a small fortune, but since our success had reached such heights and matters had almost careered out of control, this was the last Sale of Work ever held in our chapel to this day, for which I am eternally grateful!

The momentous day came to an end with a successful concert held in the chapel. We considered ourselves very lucky as a chapel in a neighbouring village had undertaken something similar to us, but with a rather unpleasant conclusion. They had been highly ambitious in inviting an important and influential celebrity from the music world to preside over their evening entertainment. The secretary's wife had taken it for granted that the gentleman would join her and her husband for a meal prior to the evening function, as was usually the case. A new and expensive tea set was bought in preparation. However, this time the wife of the treasurer had her own idea. She thought it was her duty to entertain such an important person, especially as her daughter had considerable musical talent and might in the future need such influential contacts. The treasurer himself was a very modest man and had no wish to enter into the competition, but his wife insisted and she won the day. It took a long time for the two men to settle their wives' differences and the affair had a detrimental affect on the entire chapel community.

The Sale of Work experience led me to believe that the very worst side of human nature thrives on competition, a theory confirmed on subsequent occasions. At times the chapel had to entertain large gatherings of clergy and deacons from the surrounding chapels during their Presbyterian quarterly meetings. These were held at different chapels in turns. Food, of course, was an important item on the agenda and the womenfolk of the chapels provided it. The meals were served in the vestry. Fortunately the combined desk and seat bench could, by the judicious turn of a key, be converted to make a table and a seat. Traditionally, two women were placed in charge of each table, a position which was handed down from one generation to the next. My mother had a table but surrendered it when her friend, who had shared with her, died without leaving a female successor. I was later privileged to be invited as a chosen partner of Hettie Ellen, another formidable lady in the best tradition of Blaen-y-groes.

I vividly remember one occasion, not long after the famous Sale of Work, when a very important meeting was held at the chapel. My mother, always something of a power behind the scenes, threw herself into the spirit of the occasion and was determined that our table would excel at trifles. All the important cookery books were consulted, including Mrs Beeton and Elizabeth Craig. A recipe was chosen which involved ratafia and macaroon biscuits, items which were unheard of in the local shops.

Not to be deterred by this setback, my mother managed to get hold of them through relatives living in Cardiff. It all proved worthwhile when some of the ministers at our table ate at least two trifles. Success was measured by the number of trifles consumed at each table. My mother heard, to her great satisfaction, that we had been the envy of all the others!

After this occasion, the minister, the Reverend Abel Price, exhibited a great deal of wisdom in deciding to put an end to all this childish competition, and no more possession of tables was to be allowed. From then on, all the food was to be pooled and handed out equally amongst the tables. This pleased most of us, but there were still some who preferred the good old-fashioned rivalry, who would try to place the important people together on one table and collect the best food for them.

The domestic skills upon which the women prided themselves were not just a matter of show, but could also prove useful in supplementing the family income. During the poverty-stricken days of my childhood, my mother, although not trained for the work, turned her hand to sewing to bring in some extra money. This made me very happy as sewing and cooking turned out to be the two loves of my life, and have remained so to this day. In fact, my mother had to keep a close eye on me when material was around. Many ladies insisted on the return of every inch of material left over after the garment was completed. Others, especially those who knew of my love of sewing, would leave all the bits and pieces behind, which was heaven for me. The very poor who could not afford to buy material would bring washed and boiled white flour bags for making underwear and pinafores. At the age of six I made a declaration that I was to be a dress designer, although unfortunately this was not to be. I possessed half a dozen dolls, all fairly worn and battered but in a fit state to be elegantly dressed. Whenever I took a fancy to a certain article of clothing in a newspaper, magazine or a catalogue, be it either a suit or a ball gown, my dolls would be dressed likewise in no time at all. My first primary school teacher, at an advanced age, told me that the headmaster had told her on my first day at school, 'Watch out for that one, there is a streak of genius running through the female side of the family.' The genius never materialised, and the ability to do science and mathematics seemed to be more of a hindrance than an asset, in my way of thinking, as I was encouraged as a result to forget my dreams of dress design.

I vividly remember one offence I committed as a child, for which I was physically punished and confined to my bedroom all day. We had an old coffer in one of the bedrooms and it gave me great pleasure to spend a wet afternoon rummaging through its cupboards and drawers. Every time I looked there was one piece of material in particular, yards and yards of it, which my mother did not seem in a hurry to use it. It was a beautiful bright red paisley and I often dreamt of what I could do with it. One wet, miserable winter's day the temptation proved too much and I took a pair of scissors and cut off a corner some eighteen inches square out of it. I had no idea what to do with the material, and how could I sew it without my mother seeing me. There was no alternative but to leave it folded, inside the big piece, until a suitable opportunity came along. Unfortunately for me, not long after my mother decided to use the red paisley to make a quilt. Quilt making had become another of her accomplishments. For this she used a large frame placed over the living-room table, taking over most of the room. I was now caught and in great trouble. I still have the quilt and when I look at it and see the piece sewn back in the corner I am constantly reminded of my wickedness at eight years old.

As a child I spent a great deal of my time in the box room, now our bathroom. There I found a wooden chest that had accompanied one of my uncles to America and back. This was full of books, mostly poetry, also old letters, photographs and postcards. I gained a great deal of knowledge about the family by reading them. A spare feather bed was kept on the floor so one could enjoy one's reading lying in great comfort. I could also dress up in old clothes, furs and hats kept in boxes there and admire myself in the mirror on the wall.

In the 1930s the woollen factories were flourishing in the area. Welsh wool was sold reasonably cheaply in the markets. It was a very coarse wool but had the great advantage of being different from all other wool in that it did not shrink. On the contrary, it was inclined to stretch. Unfortunately one could not classify it as three ply, four ply or double knitting, and hence it was difficult to apply standard knitting patterns to it. As a child I was made to wear vests knitted with this wool, which was still oily and a terrible dirty colour when newly bought. It was knitted in this state and there seemed to be a standard pattern for vests, which consisted of two straight pieces knitted in rib of knit two, purl two, sewn together, leaving openings for armholes and neck. Crocheting was added around the neck opening, with holes in it so that a tape could be threaded through and pulled tightly when worn. This made sure that the chest was well covered to avoid bronchitis. The garment had to be long enough to reach down to the knees, so that when worn, with the ribbing stretched across the body, it would tuck nicely inside the knickers or pants. After a few washings the vests would become whiter than white. Having started off with a vest reaching down to one's knees one could end up with it nearer one's ankles. It was then necessary to fold the garment several times around the middle. It kept off chills from the lower areas, and perhaps if women wore those vests today fewer would suffer from cystitis. It has to be said that these vests were none too gentle on the skin and caused a lot of itching, but they improved with every washing and until then there was no alternative but to suffer in silence.

Men's shirts and pants were made from Welsh flannel, woven in the local mills. Women also wore flannel knickers made to reach down to their knees. They were loose fitting with a waistband and a large opening between the legs, so that they did not need to be pulled down in order to use the toilet. There was a trained seamstress living in the village, who, somehow or other, was never able to ensure that both legs of men's pants were of equal length. Quite often these pants would turn up at our house with the wife of the new owner begging my mother to either lengthen or shorten one leg, before she dared show them to her husband. This operation, especially when lengthening was necessary, required considerable skill in order to hide the mistake. Of course all this proved very beneficial to my mother's business.

The very rich, as they do today, would dress better than the others, but there were some not so well off who tried hard to outdo their friends and neighbours. I remember a sample of coats arriving at our house, all placed flat in a big, long box, sent from a drapery shop in town on the bus. They were for the ladies living on a neighbouring farm off the main road. My mother and Aunt Nell had the time of their lives trying them on, until they were collected by the farm servant. It felt good to be well dressed, even for a few minutes in the seclusion of one's own home.

My mother, who was a reasonably good seamstress, had at the time sent for some coat material from JD Williams of Manchester, who seemed to provide the only mail-order catalogue for country folk. She bought a fawn and brown check for herself and a grey and black check for my aunt. They sent for a very smart pattern from Weldons which was advertised in the Sunday paper. It was a fitted coat with a scarf of the same material attached to the collar and thrown over one shoulder. When dressed in her home-made coat my mother visited the drapers shop that supplied the coats to the farm ladies. The owner, when attending to her needs, asked, 'Do you mind me asking, where did you buy that very stylish coat that you are wearing?' He was surprised to hear that she had made it herself.

An extremely snobbish lady with a double-barrelled name, Davies-Parry, shopped at the same establishment and she would not look at any clothes unless they were terribly expensive. It made no difference what she looked like, as long as she could tell all and sundry what a vast sum she had paid for her clothes. The staff had been told by the owner that when the lady came into the shop they were to increase the price of any item she inquired about. It was easier in those days as price tickets were handwritten in code.

I had all my clothes made for me as this made our small amount of money go further. However, a well-off but childless aunt of mine, Aunt Sally, every so often used to visit the children's department at Howells in Cardiff, give them my size and order a complete outfit to be sent to me. I remember receiving a light green coat, a white *crêpe-de-Chine* frock with red spots and a white panama hat. People could not understand how I was so expensively dressed. We had friends living some miles away with a daughter the same age as me but smaller in size, so these clothes were passed down to her. Another aunt, Mary Anne, would turn up with clothes or material to make clothes for me, all new. I was never allowed to wear second-hand clothes, but in those days when clothes were handed down to friends and family there may have been none available.

At the beginning of the century, black was always worn to funerals and to chapel as well. One had to be soberly dressed when attending a place of worship. The daughter of the house next door would turn out to a funeral dressed in black from head to toe, and wearing spectacles which she thought necessary for formal occasions. I never saw her wearing them every day so she obviously did not need them. I often wondered where she got them from, she must have been able to see with them. They were always the same pair, a very smart-looking pair of rimless glasses.

Another means of economising on clothes was to dye them. My mother had a black costume, a white blouse and a black hat bought for mourning. She had had enough of this outfit so decided to dye the blouse a daffodil yellow, together with a length of ribbon to decorate the hat. In my opinion the result looked hideous but my mother seemed satisfied. Old sheets which had already been turned 'sides to middle', and were getting beyond the stage where they could be used as sheets, were thought to have a little life left in them in parts. These pieces were dyed to make small curtains and skirts for dressing tables. Faded blouses and curtains were also dyed so that everything looked clean and bright in the spring.

Walls were papered often as the paper helped hold the poor plaster together but did not stay stuck for long. A thick paste of flour and water was used. The flagstones and tiles on the floors needed frequent washing. Some house-proud women would even get dock leaves and use them to make a crossmark on the tiles, the green sap from the leaves staining the tile and giving additional colour to the drab grey.

During the Second World War, every village was duty bound to contribute to the war effort in every possible way. We had a knitting circle held once a week in the local school, which was still a Church school, so the gentry family living in one of the smaller mansions in the area was in charge. They were now reduced to employing only one servant and a gardener. The wife, a church warden, and the daughter, a school governor, used to attend, bringing wool donated by some charity or other. They, it seemed, had never seen a knitting needle in all their life let alone used one. Knitting, according to them, was a pastime confined to the working class. In order to liaise with us Welsh speakers, they engaged an old servant of theirs who had married a Welshman. She was an Englishwoman who had learnt pidgin Welsh and was a faithful churchgoer. She acted as an army sergeant, doling out wool and supervising the work, of which she knew very little. The Welsh could be quite proud at times and not many attending approved of how the circle was conducted. They regarded this woman as an English servant who should not be allowed to give them orders. Wiser heads prevailed, however, and the ladies were persuaded to accept the regime, since it was the work which counted.

I enjoyed knitting as well as sewing and was used to experimenting with complicated patterns. My speciality was pullovers, but I was rather annoyed that all my efforts were presented to church members in the forces, since Mrs and Miss Parry Lewis were responsible for the distribution. It was not surprising that many of us were unhappy with the results as the majority of the knitters were chapel-goers.

Margaret Reynolds, a neighbour of ours, who was a retired lady's maid, believed that she should take part in the War effort, but felt it below her dignity to attend the knitting circle. She was quite prepared to knit at home, provided she was supplied with wool. I took her some navy wool with orders to make a pullover to fit a sailor with a 42 inch chest. I had no idea how proficient she was or whether she understood about tension or not and, as I was very young, I felt that I was in no position to ask any questions. I did, however warn her that the wool was thick and that large needles could be used. It was almost impossible to believe that the completed garment was large enough to fit a 60 inch chest. It was beautifully knitted and well sewn together, but the size was enormous. It was a wonder that she had not ran out of wool. She did admit, 'It does look rather large, but then men are large creatures and I did follow the pattern.' We accepted it graciously and the pullover was sent to the Seaman's Club in London, in the hope that there would be someone large enough to wear it. In due course a 'thank you' letter was received from a most appreciative Petty Officer who mentioned that nobody ever knitted jumpers large enough for him. Mercifully, Miss Reynolds never requested any more wool as this pullover seemed to be a more than adequate contribution.

Chapter 6

~ *The Bare Necessities* ~

Thus Blest in primal innocence they live,
Suffic'd and happy with that frugal fare
Which tasteful toil and hourly danger give.
> William Collins, 'An Ode on the Popular
> Superstitions of the Highlands of Scotland'.

Families were large at the beginning of the twentieth
century and the death rate was high among children.
There were no antibiotics, no blood transfusion or birth
control and there was considerable poverty. Good
nourishing food was scarce and people lived in dreadfully
crowded conditions. It was nothing for a husband and wife
with eight children or more to live in a two-roomed house
with an attic, without the benefit of modern sanitation
and with only a privy down the bottom of the garden.

Farming was a perilous occupation and many farmers
suffered dangerous accidents, as in the case of my great-
uncle Griff. He was a bachelor, who had spent many years
farming in New Zealand before returning to the same
occupation in this country. During threshing, a grain got
embedded accidentally in the corner of his eye. He was used
to looking after himself so he set about removing the grain

without asking for assistance. He believed that he had successfully done so and did not bother to mention the accident to anyone, not even Aunt Sarah who used to help him on the farm at Bwlch-clawdd. However, unbeknown to him, part of the grain had been left in the eye, which became increasingly painful. By the time he made up his mind to consult a doctor and a specialist, the eye was declared cancerous and it was too late for any treatment. He suffered constant agonising pain and although the doctor prescribed as much morphia as he thought necessary it was not enough. Griff had an old friend, a pharmacist in Cardiff, who used to send him extra dosages of the drug, quite illegally. One of the chapel deacons thought this should be regarded as 'a little help to cross the river'.

Aunt Sarah was engaged to be married at the time, but Stephen, her fiancé, called it off when he heard there was cancer at Bwlch-clawdd. He seemed to believe that the disease was contagious and that he might somehow become infected. Aunt Sarah was left without his support when she needed it most. She had been remarkably cheerful and good-humoured prior to the double blow of having to nurse her dying uncle and being deserted by her husband-to-be. Ironically, after Stephen married someone else, he himself died young from cancer. On his deathbed he was said to have cried out for my aunt, begging her forgiveness for having deserted her in his fear and ignorance.

Despite the dangers from such accidents, the real enemy was epidemics of diseases such as diphtheria, measles and scarlet fever. Tuberculosis ravaged through the population and it would prey in particular on those too young to have the stamina to withstand it. In one family of ten in the village, three fell victim to this disease. Two of them were young girls who had already started a family of their own, and the third was a schoolgirl. The mother herself died before she was forty. When babies were born so frequently, both mother and child tended to be weak and there was no chance of the mother ever being able to produce enough milk to breast-feed the baby. If the parents could afford it, they would engage a wet nurse to feed the little one, as they did for my Uncle Jim. He grew up to be a very strong, handsome boy who always had problems with the opposite sex. He was forever being teased by the family that it was due to what had happened to him as a small baby. Breast-feeding babies was regarded in those days as a means of contraception. One mother did this for three years with her child, at considerable expense to her own well-being, only to die soon after of tuberculosis.

I found an old postcard, dated 1909, sent to Aunt Nell, who must have been at home at the time, by Ianto, a neighbour who was a patient at Cardiff Royal Infirmary. I remember hearing that he had undergone thyroid surgery, which shows that some advanced treatment was available to country folk in those early days. I do not know who paid for the operation as he and his parents certainly did not have the means to do so. Although in his twenties, he had never been away from home before and his family could not visit it him as the journey to Cardiff was too far and too costly. The operation was a success, but the wound proved slow to heal and he had to receive some further treatment, which Ianto described as 'exrise treatment'. He nearly drove his poor mother insane with worry by writing home every day complaining about something or other. My mother and Aunt Nell along with other villagers kept writing letters and sending him postcards in an attempt to cheer him up, but to no avail. He was fortunate that a lady from Blaen-y-groes lived in Cardiff and did her best to raise his spirits by visiting him often. Even then, Ianto showed little appreciation or gratitude for any of the efforts on his behalf. Although Ianto never spoke anything but Welsh, he wrote in English, such as it was. This is the exact wording on the postcard which was written in somewhat forlorn fashion in 1909:

> Dear Nell
>
> I recieved your P.C. this morning and I was very pleased to have him and now that you are quite well all. I am quite well thank you but my neck is all right but that little spot is very slow yieling up. I am under exrise treatment three times a week, this is trying to yiel him up quick. Perhaps it will take a long time to yiel up again I dont know. I would like to come home before long my heart is gone very low. I am going down again to exrise to see inside if he is getting on allright.
> Thank you very mush for the picture of old Blaen-y-groes he is looking very nise, write soon.
> From your sincire friend
>
> Eanto

Despite his fears, Ianto recovered in due course and lived to a ripe old age, a highly-respected man who had become a deacon in his church.

There was very little a doctor could do in those days, apart from casting his eye over the family's food store and sometimes filling it from his own pocket. Dr Powell used to do just that. He was the local doctor and a cousin of my grandmother. He was always very annoyed that families used to dress up the dead in their best clothes and jewellery, before placing them in the coffin. He knew only too well that they could do with every penny available and jewellery could be sold to buy food in a crisis. Every wife had a wedding ring at least. Death could occur suddenly and frequently in a family and the cost of burying was not cheap even then.

Dr Powell's patience was tried greatly when he had to call in a specialist to see one particular patient who gave him cause for concern. This was a young farmer, the family bread winner, whose health was of the utmost importance. He had been taken seriously ill and according to the doctor the prognosis was not good. The consultant was to come from Cardiff and would expect to be provided with a meal during his visit. There was no standard fee for his consultancy; it would be based on the doctor's advice, taking into account the financial situation of the family. Dr Powell explained this to them and advised them not to give the impression that they were anything other than what they were: very ordinary farmers scraping a living off the land. The consultant should then be supplied with a very simple but tasty meal and there was every hope that they would end up with a small bill. Do you think for one minute that they listened to him? Instead, the patient's sisters dressed up in their best clothes and decked themselves out in whatever jewellery they had. The best goose was slaughtered for the feast, despite the fact that the money from its sale would have been very useful come Christmas. A lavish meal along the lines of a Christmas dinner was prepared, with trifle drowned in lashings of fresh cream as sweet. The doctor was dumbfounded. There was nothing he could do in the circumstances and as a result of their folly they were naturally charged the maximum fee. One excuse they gave was that they had a sister living in Cardiff whose husband was doing well. They felt they had to put on a show, just in case their brother-in-law might meet the specialist '*i gadw dignity Mari ni lan*' ('to keep the dignity of our Mari intact'). As it transpired the young man was suffering from a terminal illness and was soon dead, leaving the rest of the family in dire financial straits.

Dr Powell would often take food to some of the poorer households or would ask my grandmother to arrange some help. She would often ask him, 'How on earth do you manage to live, because your patients can't afford to pay you?' He was always prompt with his reply, 'Don't worry, Fitzwilliam and his kind keep me going,' referring to members of the local gentry. He was a highly popular doctor who was greatly esteemed by all his patients. When he died in 1917 there was a very large gathering at his funeral. People from all walks of life came from far and wide to pay their respects and bid the last farewell.

People in general tended to be kind and neighbourly and, whenever there was trouble, help was at hand. This was not a matter of individual heroism; this was the behaviour expected in society, similar to what we expect of the Welfare State today but with no payment involved.

Medicines were usually made at home from readily available ingredients. Elderflower and elderberry wine were considered beneficial for colds and coughs as my mother found once. During the terrible snowstorm in 1933, she had to go to town, some seven miles away, on very important business. It had barely started snowing when she caught the bus to go, but by the time she was ready to return the buses had stopped running, so she had to hire a taxi. This could go no nearer than two miles from home and she had to walk the remainder of the way. The fierce wind was whipping the snow into huge drifts across the road and by the time she had struggled home through it she was completely exhausted. A basin-full of warm elderberry wine was administered and, other than feeling rather tipsy, she suffered no ill effects.

It was customary to take a spoonful of salts – Epsoms or Kruschens – every day to keep the bowels active and to hold arthritis at bay. A family called the Eliases lived near by and the five children were given a dose of salts every Saturday morning. They all lived to a ripe old age, so perhaps the salts helped. To my horror senna pods was my dose, brewed into a tea with milk and sugar. Can anyone imagine anything more revolting? Just thinking about it makes me ill to this day, although it might not have been as repellent without the addition of the milk and sugar. I can remember the ritual of my mother attempting to persuade me to drink this horrible stuff when quite young. I was first cornered and then we all played games in which I was to compete for the senna with an imaginary rat, who for my part was more than welcome to it. When patience was exhausted and all other avenues had been explored, my nose was firmly seized and I was drenched like a cow. No wonder in later years that I myself felt so much sympathy for the cows I had to drench.

Goose grease was kept by people who ate a goose for their Christmas dinner, and by those affluent enough to provide a goose dinner for their tenants and servants on New Year's Day. It was rubbed on the chests of those who suffered from bronchitis or other chest infections. It was shared out amongst the sufferers during the winter months. Egg white was used to cure diarrhoea in humans and animals. When a calf suffered from this affliction, it would be force-fed eggs, shells and all, until cured.

My grandfather was a strong man with big muscular arms. When mending the roof at Glanaber, he had the misfortune to fall off a ladder and break his arm above the elbow. The doctor set it and put it in an ordinary bandaged sling, saying that there was sufficient muscle tissue in the arm to assist the bones to knit. He then told my mother that success would depend greatly on her as she would have to adjust the sling constantly and on no account let it slacken. She also had to rub the area with olive oil to bring out the bruising, for at least ten days. Very soon a black ring was seen on the skin at the site of the fracture and in a few weeks my grandfather was back at work suffering no after effects. Recovery back then depended as much, if not more, on good nursing as on medical treatment.

At that time, prostrate gland problems in men were untreatable. There were no indoor toilets, let alone a bathroom. One afternoon Dai Owen the butcher turned up at our house in a very worried state saying that Jonah Jones, his father-in-law, who lived nearby, was in terrible pain and was unable to pass water. The doctor had paid him a visit and had recommended a hot bath. My mother, who was a reasonably good nurse, having had a considerable amount of practice with her own family and neighbours, was appealed to for help. Firstly we had to find a bath. This problem was easily solved, as we had a suitable zinc tub. My mother and I carried the bath the half a mile to the cottage, where there was an old-fashioned open grate with a boiler alongside which always full of hot water. We needed the entire contents of the boiler to fill the bath and several cast-iron kettles full, heated on the open fire. By the time Jonah was lifted into the bath everyone had forgotten about the presence of a ten-year-old girl. I was so taken aback at the sight of this naked giant, screaming with pain, that I ran home as fast as my legs could carry me.

Scrofula is a disease almost unheard of nowadays. It used to run in families and was called 'The King's Evil', because of the belief that it could be cured by the king's touch. Sufferers were easily recognised by their 'cabbage ears', caused by the sores which made the outer ear look as if it had been eaten away. There were also very noticeable scars left on their necks, which were usually covered with a scarf. It was believed to affect men in particular and to cause them to become sexually voracious. A doctor related to a local family suffered from the disease and would visit one of the local beaches to relax in his time off. When he arrived, word would soon get around and every woman alone in her house locked the door and stayed indoors until the 'all clear' message was received. I very much doubt the truth of this belief as the doctor maintained a thriving, successful practice not so far away.

Another affliction which was supposed to affect men was the *afu wen* (white liver). I have no idea what it entailed, and I have failed to find anyone who does. It was said that these men could poison their wives, ultimately leading to their death. One man, James Tynewydd, who was said to suffer from this condition, did indeed lose three wives in succession. A lady who recently died, having survived until her hundredth year, was earlier in life bedridden and ailing for a period of seven years following her marriage to a man who seemed perfectly healthy but was rumoured to suffer from the *afu wen*. The couple never had any children.

Children grew up familiar with death. Most houses had a parlour in which the dead were kept in their coffins until the funeral, usually with the lids left open so that anyone who wished to could take a last look and bid farewell to the deceased. Many relatives chose to take advantage of this opportunity. I shall never forget the singing of the large gatherings at the graveside in some funerals. The hymn was always the same, a verse from David Charles's hymn,

> *O fryniau Caersalem, ceir gweled*
> *holl daith yr anialwch i gyd,*

sung to the tune 'Crugybar'. On one occasion, back in 1910, a neighbour's child died tragically young and the other children were strictly ordered not to enter the parlour where the body lay. However, one night when they knew their parents were safely out of the house, they took a lighted candle and some Demerara sugar from the kitchen and slipped into the parlour. They thought that they could revive the dead child by opening her eyes and feeding her sugar. The result was that the poor little corpse was covered in candle wax and smothered with sugar. Who could blame them for trying? It was difficult for them to understand why their little sister had to leave them at such an early age.

The Sanitary Inspector was a frequent visitor to homes where deaths had occurred. After an outbreak of a contagious disease, he would insist that feather beds were burnt, the house fumigated and its contents thoroughly disinfected. Fleas were real pests, since cats and dogs carried them and they thrived in feather beds, sucking blood from their victims as they slept. It was difficult to understand how someone from a good, clean home could be covered in flea bites, but these insects showed no respect for anyone, nor were they much afraid of Keating's powder, the only remedy available at the time. The insecticide DDT, when it appeared, seemed to be the answer to the flea problem and it has to be said that, however much harm it caused, it did exterminate the fleas. Many of the country folk were sorry to see it banned, as it had its uses.

Those who called themselves dentists in the country were extremely primitive in their methods. My mother was plagued by an ingrowing molar and a local quack extracted it from the outside of her jaw, using a massive pincers and no form of painkiller. She often wondered how she survived the ordeal, but she was left with a nasty scar. I remember, when quite young, a dentist coming to our house to hold a monthly surgery for a number of patients, all of whom were in desperate need of dental treatment. There was only one treatment available – extraction – so people naturally suffered as much as they could bear before thinking of approaching a dentist. Upon arrival, Jones the Dentist's first requirement was a bucket, half full of water. I hid in the back kitchen, but still could not escape the screams, so I am sure that nothing was used to deaden the pain. Later on things improved with the use of cocaine and later gas as a pain killer.

I can still picture the bucket with teeth floating in the bloody water as it was taken out to be emptied on the dung heap. As always, being of an inquisitive nature, I was impelled to go and examine the debris. The teeth looked huge, proving that there was more tooth buried in the gum than could be seen in the mouth. It was a nightmarish prospect: teeth brown-black with rot ending in narrow prongs with particles of flesh still clinging to them. I never heard that any of the patients suffered any permanent damage as a result of this rough treatment, but I am sure that there were many sore mouths and jaws for some time.

Jones's method was regarded as quite modern in his day and less painful than many, as it was quite common for anyone who possessed a suitable pair of pincers and a strong arm to help relieve friends, family and neighbours of excruciating pain by pulling out the bad tooth. It saved money as dentists' fees were quite substantial. The visiting dentists proved popular for many years, and it was surprising how many preferred to be treated in a room in a private house, rather than in a proper surgery after they became available.

Doctors would also hire rooms in private houses in villages in order to conduct surgeries. This was very convenient for patients, as it was a long time before people had their own transport and buses were few and far between. Doctors still hold surgeries in our village hall and it is a great help, especially for the elderly who do not drive but wish to retain their independence.

We had no indoor sanitation in Parcderyn until after the Second World War, although we did have a toilet with an Elsan which was much nearer the house than the bottom of the garden. Its proximity to the house proved to be a blessing when one had to pay a nightly visit or when the rain came teeming down. However, despite the inconvenience, I always felt that there was something very romantic about a privy down the bottom of the garden. They were usually placed in an obscure position, so it was possible to leave the door open and enjoy the flowers, the greenery and the blue sky on a beautiful spring or summer day. Admittedly it was not so pleasant on a stormy winter's night, but being able to gaze at the moon and the stars on a clear, frosty evening compensated for all the inconveniences. When we were young the cold and the rain did not seem to matter so much. We walked everywhere, sometimes as much as three to four miles one way, for our entertainment. There was always a crowd of us and the journey in company was always great fun in itself, never mind the concert or eisteddfod which was our destination. I actually cannot recollect it raining at all during my youth, until I went to university at Aberystwyth and was frequently soaked walking home along the prom!

I was well acquainted with some of the local privies and recall them clearly to this day. My friend Mary lived up the road, and their privy was a substantial stone building, with slated roof and a pigsty adjoining. The house had been the property of Glanaber House and had been well built. The pigsty next door was used to store coal rather than a pig.

The privy was a very cosy little building with a two-hole seat with lids to both, kept scrupulously clean with the walls whitewashed once a year. Toilet paper was unheard of, so the local *Gazette* and any spare paper was put to use. It could sometimes prove good reading material. Mary and I spent a lot of time here, chatting and reading. With the door open, one faced the garden hedge with an abundant growth of wild flowers. It has been said that country gardens have never produced the same high quality and quantity of crops since these old toilets, with their ready supply of manure, became obsolete.

Some time after she had been deserted by her fiancé, Aunt Sarah married a rich widower who had bought the smallholding of Coedlan after retiring from farming. This was a mini-mansion and looking back I still think that it was the most attractive house that I have ever known. Coedlan was located in an idyllic setting; to approach it one turned off a country lane along a short drive bordered by trees. The house was surrounded by a walled garden and part of the enchantment of the place was entering the garden by one of the two large wooden doors, which opened by turning a heavy metal ring. The front door also opened right into this charming garden. The privy was in the woods a little way from the house. It was as luxurious as one might expect from such a well-appointed house. My uncle was an official of the National Farmer's Union, so the literature found there consisted of NFU reports. I must say that the paper was good, it was quite thin and soft, as good as any available nowadays. Whilst seated there in complete tranquillity, reading all about the problems of the farming world, it was not uncommon to be visited by an inquisitive squirrel or maybe a pheasant passing the time of day. In the early morning it was no surprise to meet a fox. His presence caused my aunt some concern for the welfare of her chickens. I did actually see the rogue joining the hens for breakfast after my aunt had left the yard first thing in the morning, without touching one of them. But I was also unfortunate enough to witness the aftermath of a night's slaughter by a fox, when we had foolishly forgotten to close the hen house one stormy night. It was heartbreaking in the morning to see all the dead corpses which seemed to be the result of killing for killing's sake.

Another farm that I used to visit often had a unique type of privy. It was newly built, of zinc and wood, and placed over a fast-flowing stream. This must have been an attempt at modern sanitation, but what would the Rivers Authority say to this today? Looking down the big open hole was like staring into a deep cavern. It was quite fascinating, as the water seemed so far away and its speed amazed me. No doubt, there was a great deal to be said for this toilet, but it could prove rather eerie sitting there listening to the roar of the river underneath.

Nant-blaen's privy was located in the orchard. This was a lovely place, surrounded on one side by fruit trees and conifers. This was called 'the Plantation', a romantic name, although I have no idea when or why it had been thus christened. To the other side the land fell away to a lake supplied with water from a nearby field. No-one refers to the Plantation any more, and why should they, as the place no longer bears any resemblance to its former glory? The stone privy still stands in a corner where it was once overhung by an apple tree which bore sweet, red fruit.

Autumn was the time to make frequent visits to the family at Nant-blaen. It was easy enough to ask permission to make use of their facilities, to sit awhile listening to the ripe apples falling on the roof and landing near enough to be picked up and eaten.

Of all the primitive toilets I ever encountered, school toilets were truly the most horrible of the lot. There were those for the girls and those for the boys, four each in a row and placed back to back. They were usually in a dreadful state because there were so many children and the buckets were only emptied at the end of the day. Newspaper was supplied, cut into small pieces and hung from a bent skewer fixed to the wall. Between the stench and the unsavoury state of the floors, only a dire emergency would impel anyone to use them by the afternoon. The job of the caretaker was not a pleasant one, but by the morning the whole school, inside and outside, was spotless, with fires lit in winter.

Many countrymen claimed that it was better to emulate their livestock and make use of a hedgerow or a cowshed when the need arose. During long hours in the field one would have to climb over the hedge if there was no gate to the next field. There was a golden rule that men and women were not to go on such an errand at the same time. A certain etiquette had to be observed even in these matters and people were expected to obey a strict code of conduct.

Martin, our wayward evacuee, came to speak a mixture of Welsh and English during his time with us. He was up to all kind of tricks, especially if he was asked to undertake any kind of chore. One of his usual responses was to approach my mother with wide-eyed innocence announcing, 'Aunty, I must go and *agor dy drowser*' [open your trousers]. This inevitably meant a long visit to an outside toilet, not necessarily ours even, and could probably last the whole day. Needless to say, my mother was none too pleased.

The smithy next door had a toilet down the garden, but for some unknown reason the blacksmith seemed reluctant to use it. Several times a day he would pass our house and wander up the drive of Glanaber mansion. If he encountered anyone on his way, he would stand, peer up at the sky and muse, 'I wonder what it's going to do,' referring to the weather. 'I am going to see what's it like over the Frenni Fawr.' Admittedly, at one point along the drive one was able to see the range of mountains in Pembrokeshire called the Frenni. However, I doubt if it was necessary to check the weather prospects several times a day from this vantage point, but that would always be his story, despite the fact that his visits were inevitably well known in the village.

On those occasions when my grandfather did not have a great deal of building work on the go, my uncles would set off to some town or other to look for work elsewhere. There were always two things in particular that they looked forward to on their return: a visit to the privy in the garden and their mother's *cawl*. For a while after they came home it would be *cawl* for breakfast, dinner and supper until they had satisfied their craving.

Apart from occasional visits to relatives in south Wales, I only experienced the luxury of a bathroom when I went to university. I had a bath every day, as it was such a novelty to see hot water coming out of the taps so easily. It was so much easier than having to lug bucketfuls from the boiler next to the fireplace, then having to wash in not particularly hot water in a zinc bath in front of the fire, always supposing one could find a convenient time when no-one was around.

There was no council water either when I was a child but, fortunately, we had an eighteen-foot-deep well right in front of our house. I remember the bucket was let down by turning a handle and lifted up full of water. The well was round at the top and lined with stones which were supported on timbers across the bottom part which was about six foot square. A lightweight covering had been placed over the top, which our family doctor happened to notice when he called when one of my children was ill. Quite out of the blue he asked whether the well was a gimmick or was genuine. Having been told that it was indeed a real well, and a deep one at that, he went to examine it in detail and expressed his opinion in no uncertain terms.

'Don't call me when someone falls in here and drowns,' he warned.

'But our children know better than to play about around the well,' I protested.

'It won't be your children I'll have to drag out, but someone else's, who aren't used to it. Don't call me here again until you've covered that well properly.'

This ultimatum alerted us to the dangers and my husband went to work immediately to put things right.

Two hundred yards up the road there was another house which had a well similar to ours, but in the garden away from the road. As he was passing the house one day, a neighbour called Evan Tom thought he heard a very faint cry for help. He thought it best to investigate, and went first to look for the middle-aged lady, called Nan, who lived alone in Brynteg. Having failed to find her, he called out and the faint cry was repeated. He realised now that it came from the well. Nan was down there, on a ledge not far from the top where she was in no danger of drowning. He got hold of a ladder and soon Nan was rescued, dry and not much the worse for the episode. People said afterwards that it was all a stunt to draw attention to herself. She was feeling rather downhearted at the time as a certain widower who used to visit regularly had been rather cool of late and his visits had become more infrequent. It was a rather desperate action to take to rekindle his ardour.

Every year when the summer was at its driest, our well was drained of all its water and Charlie Povey would descend by ladder to clean the inside wall, which had gathered slime. He would then lime-wash it all to disinfect it. Lime was often used for this purpose. I heard it said many a time when my grandfather had his skin torn whilst working on a building site that he would dab the cut with lime, which must have burnt like the devil. Urine was also used for the same purpose. I myself saw farmers, having completed some dirty job, coming into the cowshed to wait for one of the cows to urinate and rubbing their hands in the flow to clean them.

The next advancement with our water system was a pipe from the well to a hand pump fixed to the wall by the back door of the house. I spent a great deal of my time pumping water for the house, as well as for the animals who were inside over winter. The cows had a terrific thirst, and the number of bucketfuls they drank seemed endless. When we no longer drank water from the well, the pump was moved to the cowshed. We were slowly showing signs of advancing from the dark ages. The well proved very useful during the drought of 1976. Although we could not drink it, as it had not been properly tested, it was used for everything else. Unfortunately, it finally collapsed, as the timbers rotted away over the years. As it would cost a small fortune to restore the well to its former glory, there was little choice but to fill it in. We did so with a heavy heart.

Council water came at last, in a primitive way. A cistern was built on the roadside some hundred yards from our house with a flagstone placed as a lid over it. We fetched drinking water from it daily, but still used well water for other purposes. It became a meeting-place for women to congregate, sitting on the flagstone waiting for their buckets to fill. It reminded me of the story in Genesis, where Abraham sent his servant to seek a wife for his son Isaac, instructing him to, 'Stand by the well of water, where the daughters of the men of the city come and draw water.'

There was great excitement when we heard that council water was to be provided to all householders along the main road in 1935. Taps were to be installed so many yards apart, within easy reach of all the houses. A big reservoir had to be built first on a nearby farm and the contract for the work was given to a firm from north Wales. Of course, they had to employ local labour but the expertise came from outside. The man in charge was called Bonzo, and he had what he called a 'housekeeper' staying with him. Both spoke Welsh with a very pronounced north Wales accent, which sounded rather strange to us, although we soon became accustomed to it. These two stayed on the farm close to the works, whilst the foreman, Bob, who was also the housekeeper's brother, stayed with us. I was about eight when Bonzo brought Bob to our house and explained that he was rather fond of his drink, but as he was such a nice fellow it should be easy to stop him from going to the pub up the road every night. Easier said than done. He was not too bad at the start, but one night it was getting late and there was no sign of Bob coming home. I had refused to go to bed as I was too worried about Bob's welfare. Eventually we heard someone stumbling in. I can remember the scene quite vividly: he was soaking wet, although it was not raining, in his stocking feet but clutching one shoe in his hand. His first words in a slurred voice were, 'One shoe missing. I fell into the ditch and lost my shoe and I have been looking for it ever since.' He was sent off smartly to bed and his clothes taken outside ready for the wash tub. My mother gave him his marching orders in the morning. My mother and Aunt Nell went the following day in search of the missing shoe and found it lodged to one side of the ditch running along the roadside.

The farmer where Bonzo was staying took Bob in, although he insisted my mother was making a fuss over nothing. The farm was almost two miles from the nearest village, but Bob would walk there to the pub each night. This made it difficult for him to get home, especially as he was far from sober. One night after Bob had failed to turn up at a reasonable hour, everyone on the farm went out looking for him with torches and hurricane lamps. They were afraid that that he had taken a short cut through the reservoir field and had fallen into one of the deep open trenches full of water. After a worrying night with no sign of Bob, dead or alive, they found out that a fellow worker from the village had taken pity on Bob and had given him a roof for the night. In the end he had to return home as he was too much of a liability for his sister and Bonzo and, indeed, for the entire village!

Like proper sanitation, electricity was unknown in our area during my childhood. We had to use oil lamps and candles indoors and carried hurricane lamps and torches outside. The feeble light given by the oil lamp made it difficult to read after dark. How I managed to get my homework done and study for exams I shall never know. If one wanted to read in bed the answer was a candle. I believe in my creator and more so because of the way he looked after my mother. She enjoyed reading in bed, a strange combination of a chapter from the Bible every night followed by one of my comics. She had the candlestick on the bed as near as possible to the reading material and occasionally she would fall asleep whilst still reading, with the candle still alight. On more than one occasion, she woke in the morning to find the candlestick fallen over, completely burnt out and the bedcover covered in candle wax. Somehow or other she escaped being burnt to a crisp.

In the absence of electric cookers, one either had to use the open fireplace for frying and boiling or the paraffin stove for baking. The cast-iron kettle was kept simmering on top of the oven and then placed on the fire to bring it to the boil. Coal was very expensive and the ordinary folk used culm, or coal dust combined with clay and shaped into small balls ready to put on the fire. The coal dust was quite cheap to buy, as was the clay, which could be found locally. Half a ton of each would be bought before winter and placed in mounds on the yard. Then the mixing would take place with a shovel, and, as in cooking, a well was made in the centre and water added. It was very important to mix well and not to add too much water, although the culm did dry out a little during storage. It was a big load off people's minds once the culm was ready and stored in its rightful place ready for winter. One farmer in the village, Dan Maesglas, looked forward eagerly every year to the mixing of his culm. Whilst others regarded it as a day of hard slog, he considered it a day of undiluted pleasure. He would arrange for the coal dust to be emptied on top of the clay and a calculated amount of water added in one go, then he mounted his horse so that the poor animal could undertake the mixing by trampling around in the mixture. A good many felt that clearing up the mess afterwards let alone cleaning the horse was not worth the fun. Still he thought that the yearly event was worthwhile.

The fire in the open grate was never allowed to go out, so before retiring at night a strong fire was built up to hold the closely-fitting balls of culm which were placed on top. It was a deadly sin to let the fire go out during the night. In the morning a poker was used to make a hole in the hard crust formed on the surface and soon a blue flame would appear. The poker would then be put between the bars to shake out all the ashes, the tray cleaned and a new day started afresh. Culm never gave out great heat, but it provided a fairly constant heat, and the water in the boiler alongside the grate, on the other side to the oven, was always hot. One big problem with the culm was that making the balls proved to be a very dirty process and rubber gloves were unheard of in those days. Before going out anywhere important the housewife always washed an article of dirty clothing in order to get her hands clean. I remember a friend of mine, a nurse in England, who came home to nurse her sick mother and rather than get her hands dirty making culm balls, paid her brother dearly for helping her out. With better standards of living – the introduction of the Dover Range, followed by the Triplex and finally the Rayburn and Aga for cooking, and the tiled grates for the sitting rooms – culm became a thing of the past. Wood and coal became popular as fuel for these modern open fireplaces. Wood was plentiful and most people had access to a tree, either in their garden or given to them by a farmer in exchange for work done. Neither coal nor wood or the combination of both had the lasting power of culm and the open fire could not be kept alight during the night, but this was not necessary any more with the modern range.

The food was plain and was all homemade. We had the Sunday lunch with fresh meat provided by Dai Owen the butcher, who called every Saturday. It was already packed, and the price was always fixed at four shillings and sixpence. There was obviously no inflation involved. It was sometime difficult to ascertain from which type of animal the meat originated. There was never any mention of the price per pound, the actual weight or what cut was in the wrapped greaseproof paper placed on the kitchen table every Saturday evening. Funnily enough I never heard my mother asking any questions, perhaps because Dai Owen was such a dear old soul who made his delivery in a dilapidated old van very much the worse for wear. His father-in-law, Jonah Jones, lived close by and as a child I used to fetch the old man's pension from the Post Office about a mile away, then take it over to him along a muddy lane. Halfway along the lane was a gate which seemed completely unnecessary to me. It was very difficult to open and more often than not I would have to climb over it. A piece of metal with the words 'Please shut the gate' printed on it was screwed onto the gate itself. I had so much trouble opening and closing this gate that one day, having found a nail with a sharp point to it which seemed suitable for the job, I scratched underneath, 'OK I'll shit it.' Jonah made a lot of fuss over this, wondering who the guilty person could be, but I was never a suspect, never being considered capable of such naughtiness.

As a payment for delivering the ten shillings of pension around lunchtime every week, I would be given a well earned basinful of Welsh *cawl* and a wooden spoon to eat it. His wife, Bridget, used to produce the best *cawl* in the area. The success was in part due to their son-in-law the butcher calling on Friday night with a large selection of bones. The old man was a keen gardener so the delicious *cawl* benefited also from the selection of vegetables from the garden, including leeks, of course. Jonah had been a bailiff at the nearby estate before purchasing his own little smallholding. It was often said that bailiffs on such estates became rich on their steady wage whilst the owners became poor. No doubt whisky and high living contributed to their downfall as well as other factors.

The blacksmith went to town once a week to meet travellers and salesmen from whom he bought animal feeds. He used to shop for his neighbours on these regular visits and, whatever else he bought, cutlets of hake were always included. I hardly ever came across any other edible fish, apart from herrings, which were sold by fishermen at the local beaches. Of course we all knew about the salmon poaching on the river, some distance away, but we never benefited from this.

As mentioned, neighbours were allowed to grow a few rows of potatoes in a farmer's field on condition that they helped him plant and harvest his own crop. After lifting the potatoes they were graded: the small ones into seed potato for next year's planting, the larger ones for eating and the very small ones as rejects kept for animal feed. These were mixed with swedes and mangolds and cut up for the cows and boiled for the pigs. If the eaters were in short supply, my mother occasionally scrubbed and boiled the smaller rejects in their skins. Swedes were grown on all farms and every autumn Dafydd Llan-lwyd would pass our house with a cartload to deliver to his daughter Hannah. All along his route he used to throw a few swedes into people's front gardens. They were greatly appreciated, but one did wonder how many swedes were left for Hannah by the end of the journey! It was strongly believed that swedes were very healthy to eat and that they cleared the digestive system, collecting various foul gases as the food passed along until they were eventually expelled into the outside of the body.

Cawl was an important part of the diet. A piece of bacon was cut and boiled in a large saucepan and taken out when ready. Then the vegetables from the garden – potatoes, swedes, carrots, parsnips, sprouts or shredded cabbage, leeks and parsley – were added to the liquid in the pan. The resulting *cawl* was eaten from a basin with a wooden spoon. A large quantity was made in one go and reheated on subsequent days and the taste was said to improve as the days went by. The meat, which could be very fatty, was eaten cold with plenty of pickle and beetroot when available. Bacon and eggs and fried bread with plenty of bread and butter was also a popular meal.

There was a great deal of mention about people, especially young ones, being without a 'lining'. I think it must have referred to the lining of the stomach and intestines. Uncle Griff, who lived in Cardiff, brought his children to stay during holiday time in order that they might be stuffed full of country fare, which included plenty of food fried in bacon fat. He thought that they lacked sufficient 'lining' as a result of the diet provided by their urban mother. A schoolfriend of mine was also advised by her doctor to eat more fat because he was concerned about her lack of 'lining'.

For breakfast, and when people felt unwell, gruel or flummery was eaten. This was made from oatmeal to resemble fine porridge and was eaten in the same way with sugar and milk. Oatmeal was also used for making oatcakes. Large sacks of flour were bought for bread-making and fresh yeast was available at the local shop. During the First World War ordinary flour was in short supply, so rye had to be used for bread-making. Baking took place once a week with a large number of loaves baked at the same time. A neighbouring farmer grew his own wheat, which was rather unusual in this area due to the damp climate. When I visited the farm, occasionally, the wife would present me with a loaf to take home. It looked very different from those baked by my mother. This one looked very hard and was heavy and flat, obviously made from grain they had ground themselves. Although the loaf looked highly indigestible it proved to be very tasty and one felt compelled to finish it all at one sitting.

I heard this lady, Mari Coedlas, being praised by a neighbour who thought that she must be an exceptionally good manager to raise eight children who always looked clean, well fed and well dressed. Her husband, David John, was not much help as he was given to drink and his main priority was to ensure that he himself was dressed like a gentleman. I heard that he and a friend had once gone to the local show and had spent the afternoon in the beer tent. They were overheard on the way home discussing the day's events with great wisdom and one said to the other in a very precise slow speech, 'Didn't we see thousands of people today, and isn't it funny no two were alike?' The other agreed solemnly and they spent a considerable amount of time discussing the implications of this. They say that you can only depend on children and drunkards to tell the truth.

Apart from special occasions, Sunday lunch was the only time when meat and two vegetables were consumed. When available, vegetables like cabbages, onions, broad beans, and runner beans would be boiled and smothered with lashings of butter, seasoned with salt and pepper and accompanied by an abundance of bread and butter. One vegetable at a time was cooked for a meal, depending which were in season. My favourite was boiled cabbage, especially the white heart, which had a delicious flavour.

Some years, as is still the case, mushrooms would pop up unexpectedly in the fields to add to our meals. Surplus herrings, salted and dried, were eaten as kippers. They were considered to be good for anyone who had lost their appetite and if a sow was off her food she would also be offered a kipper.

Up until the fifties, rabbits were the scourge of the farmer. They had reached such large numbers that they were consuming a high proportion of crops grown. However, they did provide cheap food for a number of people, especially the poor. Trappers were used by farmers to catch rabbits using gin traps, which are illegal today. The trappers would move from farm to farm, paying the farmer for their catch and this could be quite a substantial sum which would go some way to compensate for the crop loss that had incurred. Farmers would at times gather together, with dogs and guns, to ferret for rabbits. The problem came to an end in the fifties with the advent of myxomatosis, a cruel disease which decimated the rabbit population.

Trapping was a very unhealthy occupation as the men had to carry a heavy load of traps on their backs. They had to be out in all kinds of weather and they had none of today's protective clothing, only a woollen coat and empty sacks over their backs. As a result of their occupation many suffered from bad chests, bad backs and arthritis in their limbs. The farmers themselves set traps to catch the occasional rabbit for their own food, and some kind farmers allowed their servants to set a few traps of their own. Rabbit pie was a delicious meal. The rabbit was skinned, quartered and placed in a dish with chopped onions, carrots, parsley and thick slices of fatty bacon. Water thickened with flour was added and the dish was covered with shortcrust pastry, cooked and served hot with mashed potatoes. What was left was eaten cold for supper and was, if anything, even more delicious.

We experienced two very traumatic incidents as a result of gin trap setting. When Uncle Griff and his family were here on holiday he used to feel the urge to catch a rabbit, as he fancied a good rabbit pie cooked by my mother. On one visit, he took his daughter, Oenwen, with him to the fields to set a gin trap. Unbeknown to anyone she later decided to return by herself to inspect the trap. On hearing loud screams we went to investigate and there she was running down the field holding her arm out with the trap hanging from her index finger. She had been foolish enough to put her finger in the trap to try it out. Thankfully, no lasting damage was done.

You would think that this would have been enough of a lesson for my uncle, but no, he was soon at it again. This time on inspecting the trap, we found that no rabbit had been caught but instead a corner of an animal's tongue. We soon discovered that it belonged to our best milker, Blodwen. She looked very sorry for herself but fortunately as it had been a clean cut it had not bled very much. The vet had no magic cure but suggested that we found a cast-off horn – which cows were allowed to retain in those days – and use it to drench her with olive oil in order to keep the tongue moist. She had to be fed with milk and gruel several times a day. Any animal was too precious to lose, so we nursed her around the clock. She recovered and was no worse for her ordeal.

Another of our cows had mastitis in the days before the arrival of the miracle antibiotics. We had paid quite a lot of money for her so everything possible had to be done to save her udder. The vet's advice was to spray the udder with cold water to reduce the temperature and control the inflammation. We used a stirrup pump as it produced a strong jet of water and took it in turns all day and all night to pump the water. In two days the cow was back to normal and the milk was flowing freely from her four teats. The vet considered our triumph remarkable, as according to him the cow had suffered from a very virulent strain of mastitis from which only a few recovered.

Chickens were kept by every farm and everybody else who could lay their hands on a spare bit of land. Eggs were an important part of the diet and ham and eggs was a very popular meal. A cockerel was always kept with the hens so that they might become broody and sit on their eggs. The hen and her brood were a lovely sight. The chicks were kept so that the cockerels could be killed for the table and the young pullets reared for laying. Old hens, past their prime, were boiled for *cawl* and the meat eaten cold. The poor would buy these old fowl cheaply and they were made to feed many mouths with several nutritious meals.

Shallots were grown in the garden for making large jars of pickles. Sioni Winwns and his friends, the onion sellers from Brittany, came and took over the attic of a pub in Newcastle Emlyn, bringing their onions with them and stringing them up there. They would then tour the countryside on their bikes, selling their onions. Some had learnt to speak Welsh. There was one well-known character called Jim who returned year after year, spoke

171

fluent Welsh and would refuse to leave until he'd sold a string. Selling was a lengthy process as one had to haggle over the price. We all knew that we had lost the day when Jim started to cry in despair for his starving family at home. Nobody had the heart to continue haggling in the face of his distress. Of course, we all knew that he was exaggerating, but he also knew that his method was paying him dividends. He was their best salesman. One had to admit that their onions were good value for money, so no-one bothered to grow onions in their gardens. Jim was succeeded by his son, another Welsh speaker, but not a patch on his father as a salesman. We had a lot in common with the Bretons as they were fellow Celts.

At one time, when the cows were dry, my grandmother had to buy butter from a neighbouring farm. She found out that the farmer's wife charged a different price to different people, and that she was paying the maximum. This annoyed her immensely, but on complaining she was told, in a tone that brooked no argument, 'That's the price for you, Elizabeth.' Fortunately the cows calved and there was soon plenty of home-produced butter available.

To make butter, the milk was placed in shallow slate trays which were fixed in the dairy. When the cream had risen to the top it was skimmed off and stored, and the skimmed milk was fed to the pig and calves. Every week the cream was put in one of the large butter churns, which are sold as antiques today. The handle was turned for what seemed hours, churning the mixture until, when looking through a tiny glass window in the churn's lid, there was evidence that a solid mass of butter had separated out. Once, while my Aunt Nell was furiously turning the handle, a tiny plug flew out of the lid and hit her on her forehead. She was fortunate that no great damage was done, but she was left with a lifelong scar.

The butter was washed, removed from the churn, salt added, and then, with the use of hand clappers, made into small rectangular or round blocks of a pound in weight. The liquid left in the churn was buttermilk, which was considered nutritious and today it is sold at health-food shops as a delicacy. We used to drink it with our *cawl*. We also enjoyed potatoes mashed with a lump of butter, eaten from a basin with a wooden spoon washed down with a mug of buttermilk. Some people preferred to eat it all mixed together. The butter was sold locally at a fixed price, replacing the old system of selling butter in crocks which left farmers at the mercy of the visiting traders who paid wickedly low prices.

Salt was bought as rock salt in blocks of 28lbs once a year, ready for salting the pig and there usually was enough left to keep the household going for the remainder of the year. It had to be stored in small crocks near the fireplace to keep it from falling prey to dampness.

When I was about seven years old, a wedding breakfast was held at our house for a member of the family. There were twelve people seated around the large table in our living room. The only part of the feast that I can remember is the trifle. The glass bowl it was in was the largest I've seen to this day. I never knew where it came from or to where it went, but I do know that it was not ours. I was not allowed to take part in this function and was relegated to peeping through the door which had been left ajar, in wide-eyed wonder at such a wonderful spread. It was cruel that no-one took pity on me, knowing that I must be starving. After it was all over, Aunt Sarah, who had provided my mother with the food to cook, took all the leftovers away, and the trifle which I had yearned to sample had all been devoured. Fate seemed very cruel to little girls, and adults could be so inconsiderate.

I learnt whilst very young, therefore, that life was unfair and, like every good Cardi, I learnt to make the most of the little that came my way. However, the old Cardi and his world as I have described them are by now relegated to the pages of history. This close-knit community, with all its weaknesses, is gone forever. The pigsty is empty and the smithy disused. The ivy grew over the privy at the bottom of the garden a long time ago. The children on the yard of the village school play in English now. The characters in these tales, saints and sinners, have returned to the soil, and I doubt that we shall see their like again.